# FIFTH GRADE MATH
## Table of Contents

## Introduction

Mathematics skills are utilized in every aspect of an individual's life, whether a student or an adult. These skills, however, involve more than just the computation of numbers. Organization, investigation, logical reasoning, and communication are also basic skills associated with mathematics. Students must develop a solid foundation in basic mathematics skills in order to meet the challenges of learning. Once armed with these tools, they can face new situations with confidence in their ability to solve problems and to make decisions.

The *Fifth Grade Math* program is offered to develop and strengthen mathematics skills. Each page provides practice in one specified skill. The worksheet can be used to assess students' understanding of the concept before or after the classroom lesson, or it can be used by students who might benefit from additional practice, either at home or school.

## Organization

Eight units cover the basic mathematics skills taught in the fifth grade. Students begin with a review of place value and the skills needed to add and subtract numbers. They move on to practice skills dealing with multiplication and division. Students then proceed to explore essential skills involving fractions and measurement. Finally, the book focuses on geometry and graphs. Fun, thematic worksheet titles attract students' interest. One page at the end of each unit is devoted solely to word problems which show how the learned skill might be applied to a real-world situation. These problems also provide practice in using a variety of problem-solving strategies.

## Special Features

Each worksheet serves as practice for only one basic mathematics skill. Students who may need additional practice could benefit from these pages. Each page in the *Fifth Grade Math* book also ends with a word problem. These problems deal only with the skill students are practicing. These word problems also provide examples of how mathematics skills can be applied to the real world.

## Use

This book is designed for independent use by students who have had instruction in the specific skills covered in the lessons. Copies of the worksheets can be given to individuals, pairs of students, or small groups for completion. The worksheets can also be given as homework for reviewing and reinforcing basic mathematics skills.

To begin, determine the implementation that fits your students' needs and your classroom structure. The following plan suggests a format for use:

1. Explain the purpose of the worksheets to your class.
2. Review the mechanics of how you want students to work with the exercises.
3. Review the specific skill for the students who may not remember the process for successful completion of the computation.
4. Introduce students to the process and to the purpose of the activities.
5. Do a practice activity together.
6. Discuss how students can use the skill as they work and play.

## Additional Notes

1. A letter to parents is included on page 4. Send it home with the students and encourage them to share it with their parents.
2. Have fun with the pages. Math should be an enjoyable adventure that helps students grow, not only in math, but in their confidence and their ability to face new and challenging experiences.

Dear Parent,

Mathematics skills are important tools that your child will use throughout his or her life. These skills encompass more than just the computation of numbers. They involve the ability of individuals to organize, investigate, reason, and communicate. Thus, your child must develop a strong foundation of basic mathematics skills in the elementary grades so that he or she can expand and build on these skills to help navigate through the life experiences.

During the year, your child will be learning and practicing many mathematics skills in class. Some of the skills include multiplying and dividing numbers with more than two digits, computing fractions and decimals, and working with graphs. After exploring the concepts associated with these basic skills, your child will bring home worksheets, whether completed in class or to be completed at home, designed to further practice these skills. To help your child progress at a faster rate, please consider the following suggestions:

- Together, review the work your child brings home or completes at home. Discuss any errors and encourage your child to correct them.
- Encourage your child to make up word problems that apply to newly learned skills.
- Guide your child to see why it is important to learn math by pointing out ways that math is used in everyday life.
- Play games and solve puzzles with your child that utilize math skills.

Thank you for your help. Your child and I appreciate your assistance and reinforcement in this learning process.

Cordially,

# MATH RACE

Solve.

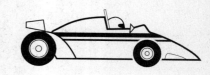

**1.**  435
  + 249

**2.**  25,901
  + 12,000

**3.**  862
  − 54

**4.**  63,014
  − 2,364

**5.**  $44.67
  + 21.99

**6.**  1.000
  − 0.001

**7.**  3.6
  × 4

**8.**  58.4
  × 37.1

**9.** 8)96

**10.**  $3\frac{3}{8}$
  $+ 2\frac{2}{8}$

**11.**  4,800
  × 300

**12.** 3)205

**13.**  $8\frac{6}{7}$
  $- 2\frac{13}{14}$

**14.**  $5\frac{4}{5}$
  $- 1\frac{1}{4}$

**15.** 65)325

**16.** 12)711.6

**17.** 7)33,950

**18.**  $7\frac{5}{6}$
  $+ 3\frac{1}{3}$

**19.** $2.34 + 9.74 =$ ____

**20.** $0.6 \times 0.3 =$ ____

**21.** $750 \div 4 =$ ____

**22.** $89 + 43 =$ ____

**23.** $99 \times 5 =$ ____

**24.** $38.60 - 12.92 =$ ____

**25.** $6,000 - 431 =$ ____

**26.** $4.56 \div 8 =$ ____

# ··· TRY YOUR HAND AT PROBLEM SOLVING ···

Choose the strategy and solve.

1. Mrs. Gonzalez buys a screwdriver for $5 and a pair of pliers for $6. She gives Mr. Miller a $20 bill. How much change does she receive?

   _____

2. In Centerville, 13.62 tons of aluminum are recycled every month. How many tons of aluminum are recycled in Centerville in 5 months?

   _____

3. A total of 428 fifth-grade students bought school pictures. If 339 students paid for their pictures, how many students must still pay?

   _____

4. A dolphin takes about 4 breaths each minute. About how many breaths does a dolphin take in 5 hours?

   _____

5. In Keith's sandwich, the meat is 8-mm thick, a slice of bread is 15-mm thick, and the lettuce is 7-mm thick. How thick is Keith's sandwich?

   _____

6. If 5 friends share 135 marbles equally, how many marbles does each person have? How many are left over?

   _____

7. The community swimming pool measures 50 ft by 25 ft by 5 ft. What is the volume of the pool?

   _____

8. The dress Sally is making requires $5\frac{3}{4}$ yd of material. She has $3\frac{1}{4}$ yd. How much more material does she need?

   _____

# ····· CHECK OUT THESE NUMBERS ·····

## Write two other forms for each number.

**1.** 102,060

_____

_____

**2.** 200,000,000 + 500,000 + 4,000 + 900 + 8

_____

_____

**3.** 100,070,000

_____

_____

**4.** 300,000 + 80,000 + 900 + 60 + 2

_____

_____

**5.** five hundred sixty-three thousand, four hundred

_____

_____

**6.** seventy million, eighty-four thousand, thirty-nine

_____

_____

## Write the value of each underlined digit in two ways.

**7.** 129,<u>4</u>15

_____

_____

**8.** <u>5</u>61,204

_____

_____

**9.** 1<u>9</u>8,975,482

_____

_____

**10.** <u>9</u>00,087,360

_____

_____

## Real World Connection

**Solve.**

**11.** When you write a bank check, you fill in the amount both in standard form and in word form. Write the standard form and word form for a check that is written for the dollar amount of 100,000 + 40,000 + 5,000 + 900 + 80 + 7.

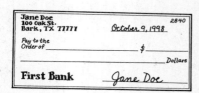

Jane Doe
100 Oak St.
Bark, TX 77777                                        2840
                                          _October 9, 1998_
Pay to the
Order of _____ $_____
                                     _____ Dollars
**First Bank**                       _Jane Doe_

_____

Name _____ Date _____

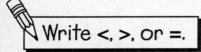 Write <, >, or =.

**1.** 1,234 ◯ 1,253                    **2.** 125,980 ◯ 124,489

**3.** 23,911 ◯ 23,918                    **4.** 546 ◯ 546

**5.** 4,122 ◯ 4,221                    **6.** 37,186 ◯ 37,145

**7.** 50,002 ◯ 50,200                    **8.** 960,435,217 ◯ 960,435,217

**9.** 2,361,528 ◯ 2,316,528          **10.** 75,948 ◯ 75,849

Order from least to greatest.

**11.** 2,345; 2,435; 2,347                    **12.** 743,194; 743,204; 753,194

_____                    _____

Order from greatest to least.

**13.** 2,345,567; 2,345,657; 2,435,657          **14.** 13,476, 13,746; 13,467

_____                    _____

## Real World Connection

**Solve.**

**15.** The 1980 census showed that Alabama had
3,890,061 people, Oklahoma had 3,025,266 people, and
Kentucky had 3,661,433 people. Order these states from
least populated to most populated.

_____

# MOVING AROUND

### Round to the nearest ten.

**1.** 34 _____    **2.** 235 _____    **3.** 450 _____    **4.** 6,257 _____

### Round to the nearest hundred.

**5.** 875 _____    **6.** 1,789 _____    **7.** 45,824 _____

### Round to the nearest thousand.

**8.** 3,457 _____    **9.** 23,532 _____    **10.** 124,890 _____

### Round to the nearest ten thousand.

**11.** 45,999 _____    **12.** 123,409 _____    **13.** 578,123 _____

### Round to the nearest hundred thousand.

**14.** 123,981 _____    **15.** 1,461,234 _____    **16.** 2,361,528 _____

### Round to the nearest million.

**17.** 56,891,789 _____    **18.** 156,148,901 _____

### Round to the nearest ten and then to the nearest thousand.

**19.** 2,346    **20.** 125,675    **21.** 1,234,499

_____    _____    _____

## Real World Connection

**Solve.**

**22.** A driver takes his truck in for an oil change every 5,000 miles. His next change will be due when the odometer reads 87,000. The odometer now reads 86,397. If the number is rounded to the nearest thousand, is the truck due for an oil change?

_____

# ··········· THE DECIMAL GAME ···········

 Shade the base-ten blocks to show each decimal number.

**1.** 0.9

**2.** 0.09

**3.** 0.009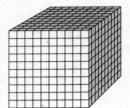

Write in standard form.

**4.** seventy-five hundredths _____

**5.** four and six tenths _____

**6.** seven and twelve hundredths _____

**7.** nine and nine thousandths _____

**8.** three hundred and five tenths _____

**9.** eight and four hundred seventy-two thousandths _____

Write the place-value position of each underlined digit.

**10.** 5.7<u>8</u>9 _____        **11.** 0.67<u>4</u> _____

**12.** 0.<u>1</u>23 _____        **13.** 3.94<u>2</u> _____

**14.** 0.03<u>8</u> _____        **15.** <u>4</u>.99 _____

**16.** 0.<u>6</u>3 _____        **17.** 7.7<u>2</u>4 _____

## Real World Connection

**Solve.**

**18.** In a survey, 1,000 people were asked what sports they liked best. Of that number, 423 said baseball and 95 said tennis. What part of total number surveyed liked baseball? What part liked tennis?

_____

# • • • • • • • • • COMPARING FRUIT • • • • • • • • • •

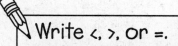 **Write <, >, or =.**

**1.** 0.87 ◯ 0.78      **2.** 12.64 ◯ 12.93

**3.** 0.851 ◯ 0.851      **4.** 1.8 ◯ 1.80

**5.** 0.06 ◯ 0.6      **6.** 258.4 ◯ 259.3

**Order from least to greatest.**

**7.** 5.12, 5.41, 5.14, 5.21 _____

**8.** 45.21, 46.89, 46.98, 45.32 _____

**9.** 0.050, 0.005, 0.505 _____

**10.** 4.123, 41,230, 41.23 _____

**Order from greatest to least.**

**11.** 0.59, 0.58, 0.63, 0.95 _____

**12.** 432.76, 532.91, 532.90, 289.74 _____

**13.** 4,968, 49.68, 496.8, 4.968 _____

**14.** 3.654, 4.356, 4.536, 3.456 _____

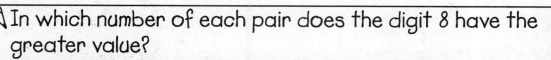
**In which number of each pair does the digit 8 have the greater value?**

**15.** 8.65 or 6.85 _____      **16.** 2.81 or 2.18 _____

## Real World Connection

**Solve.**

**17.** Which fruit costs more, bananas for $0.69 per pound or oranges for $0.72 per pound?

_____

Name _____  Date _____

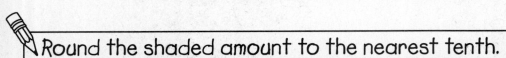

## •••••••••• THE RUN AROUND ••••••••••

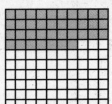 Round the shaded amount to the nearest tenth.

**1.**  _____

**2.**  _____

 Round the shaded amount to the nearest hundredth.

**3.**  _____

**4.** 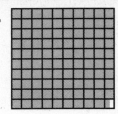 _____

Round to the nearest tenth.

**5.** 0.43 _____    **6.** 0.45 _____    **7.** 12.79 _____

**8.** 46.36 _____    **9.** 1,234.72 _____    **10.** 4,513.79 _____

Round to the nearest hundredth.

**11.** 0.123 _____    **12.** 0.148 _____    **13.** 3.547 _____

**14.** 85.612 _____    **15.** 175.431 _____    **16.** 78.465 _____

Round to the nearest dollar.

**17.** $4.57 _____    **18.** $15.19 _____    **19.** $123.79 _____

## Real World Connection

**Solve by rounding to the nearest minute.**

**20.** Jeff ran a mile in 12.55 minutes.
How many minutes did Jeff run?

_____

# ···EXPERIMENT WITH PROBLEM SOLVING···

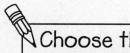 Choose the strategy and solve.

1. Phillipa wants to do a weather experiment. She walks to a store that is three tenths of a mile away to buy a thermometer. How would you write in decimal form the distance that Phillipa walks to the store?

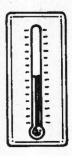

_____

2. The thermometer costs $3.42. Rounding to the nearest dime, about how much does the thermometer cost?

_____

3. Phillipa recorded the temperatures each morning from Monday to Friday. The temperatures were 67.5°F, 59.3°F, 60.4°F, 68.04°F, and 53.1°F. List the temperatures from coldest to warmest.

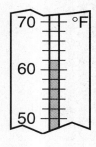

_____

4. Phillipa begins to write a report about her experiment. While doing research, she finds that the sun is ninety-three million miles away. What two forms could Phillipa use to write the number?

_____

5. When Phillipa explains her report to the class, she tells them the highest morning temperature. How would she say that number? (Hint: Read Word Problem 3)

_____

# ········ "SUM" CLOTHES DIFFERENCES ········

**Estimate the sum.**

**1.** 435
+ 241

**2.** 589
+ 24

**3.** 4,789
+ 1,234

**4.** 25,901
+ 12,000

**5.** 45,123
+ 13,498

**6.** 456
987
+ 902

**7.** 5,987
+ 2,134

**8.** 1,754
2,180
+ 1,456

**9.** 21,340
+ 794

**Estimate the difference.**

**10.** 675
– 140

**11.** 862
– 54

**12.** 825
– 450

**13.** 7,543
– 6,123

**14.** 3,504
– 283

**15.** 5,387
–1,800

**16.** 43,501
–16,789

**17.** 99,812
– 1,234

## Real World Connection

**Write the number sentence and solve.**

**18.** Jane wanted to buy a skirt for $26, a pair of shoes for $36, and a shirt for $20. She had $90 to spend. Did Jane have enough money?

_____

# •••••••••••• AIMING TO ADD •••••••••••••

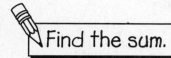 **Find the sum.**

**1.**  46
   + 14

**2.**  214
   + 117

**3.**  567
   + 253

**4.**  12
    39
    23
   + 89

**5.**  343
    897
    205
   + 134

**6.**  411
    912
    502
   + 416

**7.**  2,789
   + 1,543

**8.**  4,508
   +  932

**9.**  23,169
   +  7,548

**10.**  76,530
   + 26,482

**11.**  247,904
   + 121,865

**12.**  692,897
   + 34,723

**13.**  3,480,912
   + 2,576,955

**14.**  594,328,041
   + 305,745,932

## Real World Connection

**Write the number sentence and solve.**

15. Diego throws the javelin for his school. In three different attempts he threw 135 feet, 106 feet, and 116 feet. How far did he throw the javelin in all three throws?

_____

Name _____    Date _____

# ·········· FAN-TASTIC DIFFERENCES ··········

| Find the difference. |

1.  98
    − 14

2.  364
    − 107

3.  200
    − 123

4.  728
    − 333

5.  641
    − 259

6.  932
    − 567

7.  4,666
    − 1,888

8.  44,874
    − 12,490

9.  75,480
    − 54,371

10. 34,159
    − 19,723

11. 51,902
    − 20,921

12. 12,016
    − 6,925

13. 63,014
    − 2,364

14. 34,567
    − 15,432

15. 264,225
    − 36,004

16. 703,418
    − 520,666

17. 9,547,621
    − 9,320,858

18. 800,000,000
    − 63,275,419

## Real World Connection

**Write the number sentence and solve.**

19. A football stadium can hold 88,550 fans. If 87,650 fans attended the football game, how many empty seats were there in the stadium?

_____

Name _____  Date _____

| Estimate the sum or difference by rounding to the nearest one. |
|---|

**1.** $9.87
  + 4.05

**2.**  6.32
  − 3.91

**3.** 15.083
  − 6.568

**4.**  253.9
  + 170.4

**5.**  76.442
  − 24.031

**6.**  173.5
  + 65.9

**7.** $44.67
  + 21.99

**8.**  34.07
  − 22.99

**9.**  25.34
  + 8.68

**10.** $48.07
  − 46.92

**11.** 148.20
  + 37.88

**12.** 5,605.9
  − 354.3

**13.**  48.96
  − 38.05

**14.** 278.9
  + 36.5

**15.** $723.23 + 195.99 \approx$ _____

**16.** $8.33 - 4.92 \approx$ _____

**17.** $59.8 - 40.5 \approx$ _____

**18.** $72.30 + $15.61 \approx$ _____

## Real World Connection

**Solve.**

**19.** Steve paid $26.25 for a set of 3 CDs. Carlos paid
$24.99 for the same set at a different store. Carlos
estimated he saved $2. Steve said Carlos saved
only about $1. Whose estimate is closer?

_____

Name _____    Date _____

# •••••••••••• THE MOVIE ADD ••••••••••••

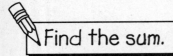

Find the sum.

**1.**  6.5
    + 3.4

**2.**  45.4
    + 7.6

**3.**  25.62
    + 10.74

**4.** 254.56
    + 45.03

**5.**  0.984
    + 0.667

**6.**  4.18
    + 0.57

**7.**  6.15
    + 3.49

**8.**  7.359
    + 5.789

**9.**  23.56
    + 12.08

**10.**  43.36
    + 9.93

**11.** 250.61
    +  5.25

**12.** 200.24
    + 152.67

**13.** 141.980
    + 259.762

**14.** 480.07
    + 297.89

**15.** 43.25 + 56.93 = _____

**16.** 0.63 + 0.43 + 1.64 = _____

**17.** 12.9 + 9.8 = _____

**18.** 35.043 + 2.865 = _____

## Real World Connection

**Write the number sentence and solve.**

**19.** Heather went to the movies. She paid $3.75 for a
ticket, $2.75 for popcorn, and $1.35 for a
container of juice. How much did she spend?

_____

Name _____    Date _____

# ········· SUITED FOR SWIMMING ·········

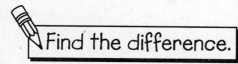Find the difference.

**1.**　5.9
　　− 3.4

**2.**　5.0
　　− 0.7

**3.**　12.4
　　− 7.6

**4.**　23.42
　　− 12.52

**5.**　4.69
　　− 4.05

**6.**　48.06
　　− 33.47

**7.**　$73.29
　　−　8.72

**8.**　30.075
　　− 30.042

**9.**　$125.73
　　− 84.29

**10.**　0.430
　　− 0.271

**11.**　836.59
　　− 416.83

**12.**　500.02
　　− 489.41

**13.**　9.405
　　− 5.766

**14.**　517.8
　　−　22.5

**15.** 5.6 − 2.3 = _____

**16.** 8.36 − 2.94 = _____

**17.** 25.641 − 7.042 = _____

**18.** 19.500 − 11.124 = _____

## Real World Connection

**Write the number sentence and solve.**

**19.** One sunsuit costs $30.45. A second sunsuit costs $17.90. How much more does the first suit cost than the second?

_____

Name _____    Date _____

# SCORING POINTS

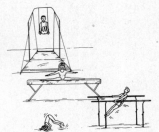

**Write two equivalent decimals for each decimal.**

**1.** 0.8 _____    **2.** 1.30 _____

**3.** 3.0 _____    **4.** 6.400 _____

**Use equivalent decimals to rewrite each problem.**

**5.** $1.2 + 4.561 = n$    **6.** $6.45 - 2 = n$

_____    _____

**7.** $8.7 - 0.02 = n$    **8.** $3.2 + 4.26 = n$

_____    _____

**9.** $25.06 - 9.315 = n$    **10.** $6.546 + 12.8 = n$

_____    _____

**Rewrite each problem. Then solve.**

**11.** $0.43 + 0.2 = n$    **12.** $0.8 + 0.52 = n$

_____    _____

**13.** $1.42 + 0.5 = n$    **14.** $4 + 23.175 = n$

_____    _____

**15.** $8.1 - 5.73 = n$    **16.** $3.864 - 0.83 = n$

_____    _____

## Real World Connection

**Write the number sentence and solve.**

**17.** A gymnast won 86.32 points for her first event,
72.9 points for her second event, and 54.8 points
for her third event. What was the gymnast's score
at the end of the third event?

_____

Name _____   Date _____

# ·············· HIVE OF ACTIVITY ··············

## Find the sum or difference.

**1.**   278
      + 154

**2.**   3.7
       − 2.8

**3.**   900
       − 86

**4.**   12.04
        28.30
       +16.15

**5.**   38.60
       − 12.92

**6.**   6,008
       − 2,419

**7.**   19.70
       + 8.93

**8.**   23.40
       − 9.75

**9.**   36,721
       − 29,879

**10.**   6.901
        + 3.678

**11.**   4.386
        + 1.245

**12.**   2.746
        + 5.987

**13.**   409,611
        − 34,909

**14.**   34,908,721
        + 12,530,563

**15.** 37,000 − 1,864 = _____

**16.** 8.25 − 7.1 = _____

**17.** 328 − 105 = _____

**18.** 80.009 − 2.451 = _____

**19.** 47.96 − 19.28 = _____

**20.** 41,523 − 2,679 = _____

## Real World Connection

**Write the number sentence and solve.**

**21.** Mrs. Lowe raises bees to produce honey. During the summer, one hive produces 108.75 pounds of honey. Another hive produces 95.4 pounds of honey. How much more honey did the first hive produce than the second?

_____

Addition and Subtraction: Mixed Practice

Math 5, SV 8049-9

Name _____  Date _____

# ·····  DRIVEN TO DO PROBLEM SOLVING  ·····

Choose the strategy and solve.

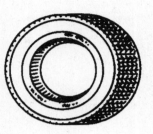

1. Ms. Ramirez buys new tires. The tires are under warranty for 35,000 miles. She has already driven 27,248 miles. How many warranty miles does she have left on these tires?

_____

2. Carl drives 36.7 miles to work. How many miles does he drive round-trip?

_____

3. Mrs. Chang used 45.332 gallons of gas in her car in September, 53.11 gallons in October, and 48.003 gallons in November. How much gas did she use in the three months combined?

_____

4. The price of gasoline at Al's Service Station is listed as $1.259. At A-One Gas it is listed at $1.199. At which station is gas cheaper? How much would you save if you bought one gallon of the cheaper gas?

_____

5. Roger is a traveling salesman. One year he drives 107,345 miles. The next year, he drives 98,416 miles. How many miles does Roger drive both years?

_____

Name _____    Date _____

# •••••••••• TEN TIMES BIGGER ••••••••••

## Use mental math to find the product.

1.  80
   × 7

2.  900
   × 4

3.  300
   × 20

4.  2,000
   ×    8

5.  6,000
   ×   90

6.  5,000
   ×   80

## Complete each number sentence by using mental math.

7. 3 × 400 = _____

8. _____ × 40 = 1,600

9. 70 × 6 = _____

10. 500 × 60 = _____

11. 9 × _____ = 5,400

12. _____ × 70 = 560

## Complete the chart.

|     | Number | Multiply by 10 | Multiply by 100 | Multiply by 1,000 |
|-----|--------|----------------|-----------------|-------------------|
| 13. | 6      |                |                 |                   |
| 14. | 7      |                |                 |                   |
| 15. | 3      |                |                 |                   |
| 16. | 50     |                |                 |                   |
| 17. | 90     |                |                 |                   |

## Real World Connection

**Write the number sentence and solve.**

18. An elephant eats about 500 pounds of food a day.
    How much food could an elephant eat in one week?

    _____

# ·········· PLANTING PRODUCTS ············

 **Estimate each product by rounding.**

**1.** 73 →
$\times\ 2$

**2.** 36 →
$\times\ 4$

**3.** 637 →
$\times\ 5$

**4.** 726 →
$\times\ 8$

**5.** 2,117 →
$\times\quad 3$

**6.** 538 →
$\times\ 6$

**7.** 5,516 →
$\times\quad 7$

**8.** 92 →
$\times\ 43$

**9.** 43 →
$\times\ 17$

**10.** 65 →
$\times\ 23$

**11.** 742 →
$\times\ 58$

**12.** 375 →
$\times\ 24$

**13.** 640 →
$\times\ 45$

## Real World Connection

**Write the number sentence and solve.**

**14.** Myrna's scout troop planted 246 tulip bulbs at their school. They plan to plant the same number of tulips at 16 other places in town. About how many tulips will they plant?

_____

Math 5, SV 8049-9

# • • • • • • • • • • PLANE PRODUCTS • • • • • • • • • •

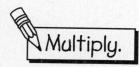 Multiply.

1.  73
   × 5

2.  58
   × 3

3.  72
   × 7

4.  302
   × 9

5.  258
   × 2

6.  142
   × 6

7.  4,106
   ×     4

8.  3,256
   ×     6

9.  5,801
   ×     9

10.  7,005
    ×     4

11.  84
   × 9

12.  6,518
   ×     7

13.  940
   × 9

14.  1,786
    ×     4

15. $7 \times 47 =$ _____

16. $6 \times 635 =$ _____

17. $8 \times 1,483 =$ _____

18. $6 \times 357 =$ _____

19. $8 \times 4,251 =$ _____

20. $3 \times 1,975 =$ _____

## Real World Connection

**Write the number sentence and solve.**

21. An airplane is flown 2,200 miles round-trip each day for a week. How many miles is that?

_____

**Multiplication: Multiplying by 1-Digit Numbers**

Math 5, SV 8049-9

Name _____     Date _____

| Find the product. |

**1.** 61
×24

**2.** 23
×12

**3.** 92
×82

**4.** 77
×27

**5.** 36
×96

**6.** 62
×45

**7.** 317
×  34

**8.** 302
×  41

**9.** 432
×  68

**10.** 501
×  65

**11.** 578
×  57

**12.** 329
×  84

**13.** 8,157
×      92

**14.** 2,786
×        43

**15.** 29 × 23 = ___

**16.** 459 × 38 = ___

**17.** 485 × 42 = ___

**18.** 953 × 67 = ___

## Real World Connection

**Write the number sentence and solve.**

**19.** The buses that take the football players to the games each holds 40 players. If there are 15 buses going to the game, what is the greatest number of players that can go by bus?

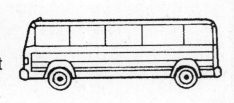

_____

Name _____    Date _____

# • • • • • • • • • • • NEWS NUMBERS • • • • • • • • • • •

 Find the product.

1.  234
   × 323

2.  732
   × 487

3.  706
   × 537

4.  749
   × 594

5.  559
   × 438

6.  584
   × 371

7.  563
   × 384

8.  264
   × 846

9.  508
   × 739

10.  379
    × 218

11.  4,597
    ×   471

12.  3,084
    ×   532

13.  9,624
    ×   248

14.  7,246
    ×   342

## Real World Connection

**Write the number sentence and solve.**

**15.** Wes has 246 customers on his paper route. How many papers does he deliver in one year?

_____

Name _____     Date _____

# •••••••••• GET TO THE POINT ••••••••••

 **Complete the pattern.**

**1.** 1 x 0.13 = 0.13
10 x 0.13 = $n$
100 x 0.13 = 13.0
1,000 x 0.13 = 130.0
$n$ = _____

**2.** 1 x 3.14 = 3.14
10 x 3.14 = 31.4
100 x 3.14 = $n$
1,000 x 3.14 = 3,140.0
$n$ = _____

 **Find each product.**

**3.** 1 x 42.3 = _____
10 x 42.3 = _____
100 x 42.3 = _____
1,000 x 42.3 = _____

**4.** 1 x 7.81 = _____
10 x 7.81 = _____
100 x 7.81 = _____
1,000 x 7.81 = _____

**Multiply each number by 10, 100, and 1,000.**

**5.** 0.3

**6.** 6.2

**7.** 8.04

**8.** 1.31

_____     _____     _____     _____

 **Find each product.**

**9.** 10 x 0.7 = _____

**10.** 100 x 0.4 = _____

**11.** 10 x 1.94 = _____

**12.** 100 x 65.1 = _____

**13.** 10 x 49.2 = _____

**14.** 100 x 80.33 = _____

## Real World Connection

**Write the number sentence and solve.**

**15.** John lives on a peninsula. The point is 6.7 miles from his house. If he sails to the point 10 times in a month, how far does John sail in a month?

_____

**Multiplication: Multiplying Decimals**

Math 5, SV 8049-9

# ··········· COMPUTER TIMES ············

**Estimate each product by rounding to the nearest whole number.**

**1.** 3.6 → ____
  × 19

**2.** 9.9 → ____
  × 34

**3.** 0.89 → ____
  × 16

**4.** 1.92 → ____
  × 56

**5.** 3.43 → ____
  × 96

**6.** 5.64 → ____
  × 17

**7.** $5.2 \times 39 \approx$ _____

**8.** $8.3 \times 44 \approx$ _____

**9.** $4.7 \times 66 \approx$ _____

**10.** $83 \times 3.14 \approx$ _____

**11.** $4.57 \times 62 \approx$ _____

**12.** $3.62 \times 96 \approx$ _____

**13.** $9.42 \times 16 \approx$ _____

**14.** $96 \times .023 \approx$ _____

**15.** $4.82 \times 47 \approx$ _____

**Because of mistakes in pressing the keys, the answer in a calculator display may not be reasonable. Estimate each product. Write R for each display that is reasonable. If the display is unreasonable, write the number and place the decimal correctly.**

**16.** $5 \times 3.62$

| 1.81 |  ____

**17.** $7.21 \times 9$

| 64.89 |  ____

**18.** $32 \times 6.37$

| 2038.4 |  ____

**19.** $62 \times 7.11$

| 440.82 |  ____

**20.** $96 \times 8.79$

| 843.84 |  ____

**21.** $2.83 \times 39$

| 1103.7 |  ____

## Real World Connection

**Write the number sentence and estimate to solve.**

**22.** Joyce can type 52.6 words per minute. Estimate how many words she can type in 6 minutes.

_____

• • • • • • • • • • • • • **POTS AND DOTS** • • • • • • • • • • • •

 Multiply. Use the model to help you.

**1.**
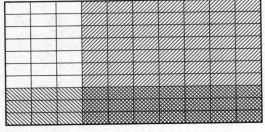

$0.3 \times 0.7 =$ _____

**2.**
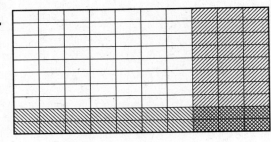

$0.2 \times 0.3 =$ _____

 Make a model to show each product.

**3.**
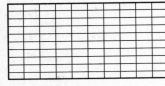

$0.7 \times 0.3 = n$

_____

**4.**
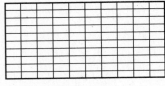

$0.5 \times 0.9 = n$

_____

**5.**
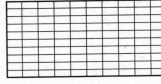

$0.5 \times 0.7 = n$

_____

Use multiplication to find each product.

**6.** $0.3 \times 0.2 =$ _____   **7.** $0.6 \times 0.3 =$ _____   **8.** $0.4 \times 0.5 =$ _____

**9.** $0.8 \times 0.9 =$ _____   **10.** $0.7 \times 0.4 =$ _____   **11.** $0.1 \times 0.9 =$ _____

## Real World Connection

**Write the number sentence and solve.**

**12.** A potter wants to make a bowl with a wall 0.4 inches thick. During heating in a kiln, the walls lose half of their thickness. How thick should the wall of the bowl be before the bowl is heated?

_____

Name _____ Date _____

# ······· MARATHON MULTIPLICATION ·······

Write the product with the *decimal point* in the correct place.

**1.** 5.2
× 7
364

_____

**2.** 3.14
× 8
2512

_____

**3.** $6.13
× 13
$7969

_____

Find the product.

**4.** 6.4
× 5

**5.** $12.31
× 4

**6.** 4.31
× 25

**7.** $4.99
× 30

**8.** 0.989
× 27

**9.** $8.21
× 21

**10.** $6.85
× 63

**11.** 4.8
× 13

**12.** 4 × 12.6 _____

**13.** 24 × $1.29 _____

**14.** 9 × 1.034 _____

**15.** 31 × 41.96 _____

## Real World Connection

**Write the number sentence and solve.**

**16.** The length of the Boston Marathon is about 26 miles. A mile is equal to 1.609 kilometers. How many kilometers does a runner cover if he or she completes the race?

_____

Name _____  Date _____

# PROBLEMS TO RECYCLE

## Find the product.

| | | |
|---|---|---|
| **1.**  1.4<br>× 0.7 | **2.**  3.2<br>× 0.9 | **3.**  6.3<br>× 3.7 |

| | | |
|---|---|---|
| **4.**  4.72<br>× 6.2 | **5.**  7.48<br>× 5.3 | **6.**  5.38<br>× 7.6 |

| | | | |
|---|---|---|---|
| **7.**  29.8<br>× 4.4 | **8.**  712.5<br>× 0.016 | **9.**  $32.93<br>×    3.7 | **10.**  512.3<br>×   2.7 |

| | | | |
|---|---|---|---|
| **11.**  0.03<br>×  0.6 | **12.**  2.07<br>× 6.5 | **13.**  4.8<br>× 13 | **14.**  4.002<br>×    15 |

**15.** 1.6 × 0.8 = _____

**16.** 9.3 × 4.2 = _____

**17.** 0.004 × 25 = _____

**18.** 3.5 × 4.17 = _____

**19.** 392.4 × 2.7 = _____

**20.** 6.39 × 2.6 = _____

## Real World Connection

**Write the number sentence and solve.**

**21.** In Centerville, 13.62 tons of aluminum are recycled every month. How many tons of aluminum are recycled in Centerville in 5 months?

_____

# • • • • • • • • • • • • • STAMP ACT • • • • • • • • • • • • •

## Find the product.

**1.**  258
    × 2

**2.**   35
    × 76

**3.**  128
    × 57

**4.**  .5
    × 7

**5.**  $1.05
    ×  6

**6.**  1.4
    × 1.4

**7.**  1,065
    ×  4

**8.**  0.09
    × 0.1

**9.**  4,824
    ×  10

**10.**  5.468
    ×  23

**11.**  $7.34
    ×  5

**12.**  2,222
    ×  957

**13.**  392.4
    ×  2.7

**14.**  $9.40
    ×  6

**15.**  0.05 × 0.3 = _____

**16.**  4,500 × 80 = _____

**17.**  1,040 × 32 = _____

**18.**  $10.95 × 21 = _____

## Real World Connection

**Write the number sentence and solve.**

**19.** Viet mails 9 postcards. Each card costs 29 cents to mail. How much does Viet spend to mail all the cards?

_____

29¢

# ·········· MULTIPLY THE SHOPPING ··········

**Choose the strategy and solve.**

1. On an average day, the Best Shop Grocery has 3,045 shoppers. How many people visit the store in October? (Hint: October has 31 days.)

_____

2. Mr. Salazar earns $9.35 per hour working in a camping equipment store. How much does he earn working 8 hours a day?

_____

3. Claire buys 1 pound of apples for $1.29 and 2 pounds of bananas for $0.91. How much tax will Claire pay if sales tax is $0.05 on each dollar? How much will Claire pay total?

_____

4. Nyrik works 40 hours a week. How many hours does he work in 8 weeks?

_____

5. Maurice earns $12 an hour for cleaning a furniture store. When he works more than 8 hours in a day, he is paid for the extra time at 1.5 times his regular rate. If Maurice works 9.25 hours on Monday, 6 hours on Tuesday, and 8.75 hours on Wednesday, how much money does he earn for those three days?

_____

Name _____   Date _____

# •••••••••• DIVIDING INTO GROUPS ••••••••••

**Choose the better estimate. Circle a or b.**

**1.** $55 \div 7 \approx n$    **2.** $281 \div 9 \approx n$

   **a.** 7   **b.** 8       **a.** 31   **b.** 32

**3.** $598 \div 8 \approx n$    **4.** $728 \div 9 \approx n$

   **a.** 75   **b.** 76       **a.** 82   **b.** 81

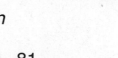

**Estimate each quotient.**

**5.** $3\overline{)23}$    **6.** $4\overline{)53}$    **7.** $6\overline{)44}$    **8.** $8\overline{)47}$

**9.** $5\overline{)53}$    **10.** $2\overline{)75}$    **11.** $9\overline{)146}$    **12.** $7\overline{)541}$

**13.** $5\overline{)453}$    **14.** $5\overline{)552}$    **15.** $4\overline{)320}$    **16.** $3\overline{)320}$

**17.** $48 \div 7 =$ _____    **18.** $37 \div 4 =$ _____    **19.** $69 \div 8 =$ _____

**20.** $135 \div 6 =$ _____    **21.** $343 \div 3 =$ _____    **22.** $553 \div 6 =$ _____

**23.** $832 \div 9 =$ _____    **24.** $569 \div 9 =$ _____    **25.** $983 \div 9 =$ _____

## Real World Connection

**Write a number sentence and estimate to solve.**

**26.** Some teachers are taking a group of 63 students to the museum. If there are 4 teachers, estimate how many students will go with each teacher.

_____

Name _____    Date _____

 · · · · · · · · · · · **IT'S SHOW TIME!** · · · · · · · · · · · · ·

**Find the quotient.**

**1.** 5)‾37̅ ___     **2.** 2)‾23̅ ___     **3.** 5)‾62̅ ___

**4.** 7)‾69̅ ___     **5.** 9)‾91̅ ___     **6.** 6)‾51̅ ___

**7.** 5)‾24̅     **8.** 7)‾67̅     **9.** 6)‾74̅     **10.** 9)‾93̅     **11.** 4)‾87̅

**12.** 5)‾65̅     **13.** 3)‾89̅     **14.** 3)‾49̅     **15.** 6)‾72̅     **16.** 4)‾94̅

**17.** 45 ÷ 8 = ___     **18.** 34 ÷ 4 = ___     **19.** 54 ÷ 5 = ___     **20.** 82 ÷ 9 = ___

**21.** 86 ÷ 8 = ___     **22.** 47 ÷ 8 = ___     **23.** 13 ÷ 9 = ___     **24.** 96 ÷ 8 = ___

## Real World Connection

**Write the number sentence and solve.**

**25.** Maria's class sold 88 tickets to a show. Each of the 22 students sold the same number of tickets. How many tickets did each one sell?

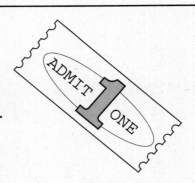

_____

# GOING FISHING

 **Divide.**

**1.** 4)360

**2.** 4)812

**3.** 6)605

**4.** 7)542

**5.** 8)638

**6.** 3)461

**7.** 7)874

**8.** 5)783

**9.** 7)3,382

**10.** 4)18,948

**11.** 3)52,654

**12.** $156 \div 7 = n$

**13.** $189 \div 8 = n$

**14.** $430 \div 4 = n$

_____

_____

_____

**15.** $593 \div 7 = n$

**16.** $5,321 \div 9 = n$

**17.** $49,327 \div 7 = n$

_____

_____

_____

## Real World Connection

**Write the number sentence and solve.**

**18.** Suki went on a fishing trip. There were 132 people waiting for 4 fishing boats. If the people were divided equally among the boats, how many went on each boat?

_____

Name _____  Date _____

## • • • • • • • • • • • • • DIVISION TABLES • • • • • • • • • • • • •

Find the quotient.

**1.** 30$\overline{)60}$          **2.** 10$\overline{)70}$          **3.** 40$\overline{)80}$

**4.** 30$\overline{)900}$         **5.** 60$\overline{)120}$         **6.** 50$\overline{)250}$

**7.** 10$\overline{)1,000}$        **8.** 30$\overline{)2,100}$        **9.** 20$\overline{)8,000}$          **10.** 30$\overline{)60,000}$

Estimate the quotient.

**11.** 16$\overline{)157}$ $\longrightarrow$ _____          **12.** 63$\overline{)433}$ $\longrightarrow$ _____

**13.** 53$\overline{)237}$ $\longrightarrow$ _____          **14.** 22$\overline{)813}$ $\longrightarrow$ _____

**15.** 17$\overline{)8,200}$ $\longrightarrow$ _____        **16.** 73$\overline{)5,575}$ $\longrightarrow$ _____

## Real World Connection

**Write the number sentence and estimate to solve.**

**17.** A cafeteria has 64 large tables. During one lunch hour, 593 students were sitting in the cafeteria. About how many students could sit at each table?

_____

Name _____    Date _____

# SOCK IT TO DIVISION

**Divide. Check with multiplication.**

**1.** $21\overline{)42}$  Check       **2.** $35\overline{)65}$  Check

**3.** $17\overline{)85}$  Check       **4.** $23\overline{)72}$  Check       **5.** $51\overline{)70}$  Check

**6.** $33\overline{)98}$  Check       **7.** $25\overline{)80}$  Check       **8.** $41\overline{)95}$  Check

**9.** $11\overline{)75}$  Check       **10.** $50\overline{)79}$  Check       **11.** $62\overline{)78}$  Check

**Find the quotient.**

**12.** $89 \div 30 =$ _____       **13.** $66 \div 13 =$ _____       **14.** $48 \div 20 =$ _____

**15.** $59 \div 19 =$ _____       **16.** $80 \div 17 =$ _____       **17.** $97 \div 44 =$ _____

## Real World Connection

**Write the number sentence and solve.**

**18.** Alana wants to buy socks. She has $11, and the socks cost $3 per pair. How many pairs of socks can Alana buy? How much money will she have left?

_____

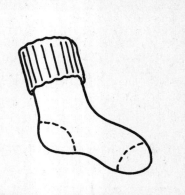

# ········· SPOONING UP DIVISION ·········

 Find the quotient.

**1.** 22)874          **2.** 35)852          **3.** 17)849

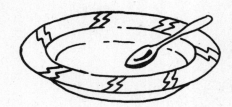

**4.** 27)570          **5.** 17)527          **6.** 34)283

**7.** 46)174          **8.** 65)325          **9.** 51)757          **10.** 19)1,729

**11.** 27)1,053     **12.** 33)3,069     **13.** 49)58,849     **14.** 50)35,010

## Real World Connection

**Write the number sentence and solve.**

**15.** Roberta has 120 spoons in her collection. She wants to buy display cases for them. She saw a case that can hold 42 spoons. How many cases would she need to hold all the spoons? How many more spoons would Roberta need to fill all the cases?

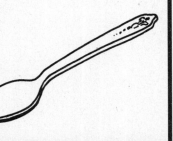

_____

# •••••••• DRESSED FOR DIVISION ••••••••

## Use mental math to complete each pattern.

**1.** 617 ÷ 10 = _____
617 ÷ 100 = 6.17

**2.** 3.6 ÷ 10 = 0.36
3.6 ÷ 100 = _____

**3.** 31.1 ÷ 10 = 3.11
31.1 ÷ 100 = _____

**4.** 6.25 ÷ 10 = _____
6.25 ÷ 100 = .0625

## Divide each number by 10, 100, and 1,000.

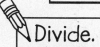

|      | Number | Divide by 10 | Divide by 100 | Divide by 1,000 |
|------|--------|--------------|---------------|-----------------|
| **5.** | 37     |              |               |                 |
| **6.** | 211    |              |               |                 |
| **7.** | 2,934  |              |               |                 |

## Divide.

**8.** 3.9 ÷ 10 = ____    **9.** 74 ÷ 10 = ____    **10.** 211 ÷ 100 = ____

**11.** 21.7 ÷ 100 = ____    **12.** 513 ÷ 100 = ____    **13.** 928 ÷ 1,000 = ____

**14.** 6.4 ÷ 10 = ____    **15.** 37 ÷ 10 = ____    **16.** 127 ÷ 100 = ____

**17.** 81.6 ÷ 100 = ____    **18.** 1,024 ÷ 100 = ____    **19.** 431 ÷ 1,000 = ____

## Real World Connection

**Write the number sentence and solve.**

**20.** Ms. Van receives an order to sew 10 costumes that are the same style and size. She buys 38.9 yards of fabric. How much fabric does each costume need?

_____

Name _____  Date _____

# ·········· IN THE DOGHOUSE ··········

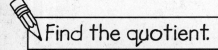Find the quotient.

**1.** $6\overline{)4.2}$    **2.** $7\overline{)2.8}$    **3.** $6\overline{)4.8}$

**4.** $9\overline{)0.27}$    **5.** $3\overline{)1.26}$    **6.** $2\overline{)6.18}$

**7.** $5\overline{)5.25}$    **8.** $4\overline{)30.4}$    **9.** $7\overline{)9.17}$    **10.** $5\overline{)40.15}$    **11.** $6\overline{)44.4}$

**12.** $14\overline{)100.8}$    **13.** $21\overline{)277.2}$    **14.** $31\overline{)164.3}$    **15.** $68\overline{)0.816}$    **16.** $12\overline{)711.6}$

**17.** $7.36 \div 2 =$ _____    **18.** $6.15 \div 3 =$ _____    **19.** $7.92 \div 6 =$ _____

**20.** $6.68 \div 4 =$ _____    **21.** $2.04 \div 6 =$ _____    **22.** $4.56 \div 8 =$ _____

## Real World Connection

**Write the number sentence and solve.**

**23.** Kevin is building a doghouse. For the trim around the roof, he bought 4 pieces of wood for a total of $6.52. How much was each piece of trim?

_____

**Division: Dividing Decimals by Whole Numbers**

Math 5, SV 8049-9

Name _____  Date _____

# •••••••• "KNOT" A PROBLEM ••••••••

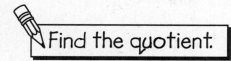 Find the quotient:

**1.** $20\overline{)40}$    **2.** $17\overline{)85}$    **3.** $11\overline{)93}$

**4.** $2\overline{)6.2}$    **5.** $7\overline{)2.8}$    **6.** $27\overline{)570}$

**7.** $6\overline{)44.4}$    **8.** $5\overline{)11.50}$    **9.** $3\overline{)5.25}$    **10.** $3\overline{)912}$    **11.** $11\overline{)1,111}$

**12.** $11\overline{)7,934}$    **13.** $48\overline{)993}$    **14.** $63\overline{)6,552}$    **15.** $27\overline{)18,927}$    **16.** $47\overline{)43,240}$

**17.** $65 \div 13 =$ _____    **18.** $549 \div 9 =$ _____    **19.** $0.98 \div 10 =$ _____

**20.** $2.04 \div 6 =$ _____    **21.** $155.16 \div 12 =$ _____    **22.** $896 \div 28 =$ _____

## Real World Connection

**Write the number sentence and solve.**

**23.** John buys rope that is 36 feet long. He cuts it into 12 equal pieces so his scout troop can practice tying different kinds of knots. How long is each piece of rope?

_____

Name _____  Date _____

# ··········· DIVISION ON THE TRAIL ··········

**Choose the strategy and solve.**

1. During his vacation, Mr. Weiss will hike 152 miles along the Appalachian Trail. He plans to walk the same distance each day. How far will Mr. Weiss hike daily to complete the hike in 8 days?

_____

2. Pete checked the prices of trail food at two stores. At Purity it cost $1.69 per package and at Supreme's it cost $4.19 for 2 packages. At which store would Pete get the better deal?

_____

3. Cabins at the Mountain Ridge Camp hold 25 people. During one week, 156 people registered to attend. How many cabins will be needed to house all the people?

_____

4. On a family backpacking trip, Fred and Jenna will carry their own clothes, a sleeping bag, and all the food for the family. Their clothes and sleeping bag weigh 18.9 pounds. The total food weight is 16 pounds. If Fred and Jenna equally share the weight of the food, will their packs be 25 pounds or less?

_____

5. At ABC Auto Supply, the cost of 6 flashlight batteries is $8.34. Smitty has only $3.00. How many batteries can he buy with this money? How much money will he have left over?

_____

## •••••••••• APPLE FRACTIONS ••••••••••

 **Write the fraction for the part that is shaded.**

**1.**  _____

**2.** _____

**3.**  _____

**4.** _____

 **Draw two pictures for each fraction. Show part of a whole with one picture and part of a group with the other picture.**

**5.** $\frac{5}{8}$

**6.** $\frac{4}{7}$

**Complete each sentence by using a fraction.**

**7.** June, July, and August are _____ of a year.

**8.** The letters *N* and *E* are _____ of the name, *New York*.

## Real World Connection

**Solve.**

**9.** Joyce ate 2 apples today. If she eats a total of 11 apples in a week, what fraction of the apples did she eat today?

_____

Name _____    Date _____

## • • • • • • • • • SAME NAME FRACTIONS • • • • • • • • •

 Write the equivalent fractions for each pair of pictures.

**1.**

_____

**2.**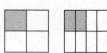

_____

**3.**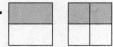

_____

**4.**

_____

 Find the missing numerator or denominator.

**5.** $\dfrac{1}{3} = \dfrac{\Box}{9}$

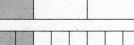

**6.** $\dfrac{\Box}{4} = \dfrac{6}{8}$

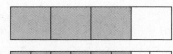

**7.** $\dfrac{3}{5} = \dfrac{6}{\Box}$

 Which fraction is not equivalent to the given fraction?
Write **a**, **b**, or **c**.

**8.** $\dfrac{1}{3}$    **a.** $\dfrac{2}{6}$    **b.** $\dfrac{3}{9}$    **c.** $\dfrac{4}{10}$    _____

**9.** $\dfrac{3}{5}$    **a.** $\dfrac{9}{15}$    **b.** $\dfrac{6}{9}$    **c.** $\dfrac{6}{10}$    _____

**10.** $\dfrac{2}{3}$    **a.** $\dfrac{6}{12}$    **b.** $\dfrac{4}{6}$    **c.** $\dfrac{8}{12}$    _____

## Real World Connection

**Solve.**

**11.** Myra's cat had 2 gray kittens, 1 white kitten, and 1 black kitten. Myra said that $\frac{1}{2}$ of the kittens were gray. Was Myra correct? Why or why not?

_____

Name _____    Date _____

# ·········· LOOK FOR THE FACTS ··········

 List the factors of each number.

**1.** 14                    **2.** 13

_____          _____

_____          _____

**3.** 36                    **4.** 32

_____          _____

 List the factors of each number. Write the common factors for each pair of numbers.

**5.** 8, 16          **6.** 9, 24          **7.** 10, 15          **8.** 12, 13

8: _____          9: _____          10: _____          12: _____

16: _____         24: _____         15: _____

_____      _____      _____         13: _____

_____

List the factors of each number. Write the greatest common factor for each pair of numbers.

**9.** 9, 27          **10.** 12, 18          **11.** 13, 39          **12.** 14, 21

_____      _____      _____      _____

_____      _____      _____      _____

## Real World Connection

**Solve.**

**13.** Chad and Xing are playing a math game with cards. Chad draws a 4 and Xing draws an 8. They decide the greatest common factor of the numbers is 2. Are they correct?

_____

**Fractions: Common Factors**

# • • • • • • • • • • • • • SIMPLY MUSIC • • • • • • • • • • • • •

**Tell whether the fraction is in simplest form. Write *yes* or *no*.**

1. $\frac{2}{3}$          2. $\frac{4}{6}$          3. $\frac{3}{5}$

_____      _____      _____

4. $\frac{7}{9}$          5. $\frac{6}{9}$          6. $\frac{9}{12}$

_____      _____      _____

**Write in simplest form.**

7. $\frac{3}{15}$     8. $\frac{4}{20}$     9. $\frac{15}{25}$     10. $\frac{12}{36}$     11. $\frac{7}{21}$

_____   _____   _____   _____   _____

12. $\frac{9}{18}$    13. $\frac{4}{24}$    14. $\frac{12}{18}$    15. $\frac{14}{16}$    16. $\frac{5}{15}$

_____   _____   _____   _____   _____

## Real World Connection

**Solve.**

17. There were 10 guitars, 20 drums, and 5 violins in a store that sells musical instruments. Write in simplest form the fraction of all the instruments that were guitars.

_____

Name _____     Date _____

# ·········· STRINGS OF MULTIPLES ··········

**Use geometric shapes, draw a number line, or list multiples to solve.**

1. Name three multiples of 4 greater than 0. _____

2. Name three multiples of 5 greater than 0. _____

3. Name two multiples of 3 that are also multiples of 4. _____

4. Name two common multiples of 9 and 2. _____

**Find the least common multiple.**

**5.** 4, 16          **6.** 2, 5          **7.** 5, 15          **8.** 6, 12          **9.** 5, 3

_____          _____          _____          _____          _____

**10.** 3, 6          **11.** 5, 9          **12.** 4, 10          **13.** 4, 12          **14.** 9, 10

_____          _____          _____          _____          _____

**Find the least common multiple of the denominators in each fraction pair.**

**15.** $\frac{1}{5}$, $\frac{1}{3}$     **16.** $\frac{1}{4}$, $\frac{4}{10}$     **17.** $\frac{2}{9}$, $\frac{1}{6}$     **18.** $\frac{3}{6}$, $\frac{1}{5}$

_____          _____          _____          _____

**19.** $\frac{3}{8}$, $\frac{1}{5}$     **20.** $\frac{2}{9}$, $\frac{1}{18}$     **21.** $\frac{3}{7}$, $\frac{1}{5}$     **22.** $\frac{1}{2}$, $\frac{7}{8}$

_____          _____          _____          _____

## Real World Connection

**Solve.**

**23.** Hester wants to make a bead bracelet. She plans to use only black and white beads. She has 12 black beads and 9 white beads. She wants to use as many beads as she can. If she uses the same number of each color of bead, what is the least number of beads she can use in her necklace?

_____

Name _____ Date _____

# • • • • • • • • • • MORE OR LESS • • • • • • • • • •

**Write two fractions greater than the one given.**

**1.** $\frac{1}{2}$      **2.** $\frac{3}{4}$      **3.** $\frac{1}{8}$

_____  _____  _____

**Compare. Write <, >, or =.**

**4.** $\frac{1}{3}$ ◯ $\frac{2}{6}$    **5.** $\frac{1}{3}$ ◯ $\frac{2}{3}$    **6.** $\frac{2}{3}$ ◯ $\frac{5}{6}$

**7.** $\frac{5}{6}$ ◯ $\frac{3}{4}$    **8.** $\frac{2}{4}$ ◯ $\frac{3}{4}$    **9.** $\frac{1}{2}$ ◯ $\frac{3}{6}$

**10.** $\frac{1}{2}$ ◯ $\frac{3}{8}$    **11.** $\frac{6}{8}$ ◯ $\frac{3}{4}$    **12.** $\frac{3}{8}$ ◯ $\frac{4}{16}$    **13.** $\frac{2}{5}$ ◯ $\frac{4}{10}$

**14.** $\frac{4}{5}$ ◯ $\frac{3}{5}$    **15.** $\frac{5}{6}$ ◯ $\frac{1}{2}$    **16.** $\frac{5}{12}$ ◯ $\frac{8}{9}$    **17.** $\frac{2}{4}$ ◯ $\frac{1}{2}$

**Write in order from least to greatest.**

**18.** $\frac{1}{3}$ , $\frac{3}{6}$ , $\frac{2}{3}$     **19.** $\frac{6}{8}$ , $\frac{1}{8}$ , $\frac{2}{4}$     **20.** $\frac{7}{12}$ , $\frac{1}{2}$ , $\frac{1}{4}$

_____  _____  _____

**Write in order from greatest to least.**

**21.** $\frac{4}{15}$ , $\frac{2}{5}$ , $\frac{1}{3}$     **22.** $\frac{5}{16}$ , $\frac{1}{4}$ , $\frac{3}{8}$     **23.** $\frac{1}{2}$ , $\frac{4}{5}$ , $\frac{9}{10}$

_____  _____  _____

## Real World Connection

**Solve.**

**24.** Rob made some fruit sauce for his pancakes. He used $\frac{3}{5}$ cup of strawberries and $\frac{7}{10}$ cup of blueberries. Did he use more strawberries or more blueberries?

_____

# • • • • • • • "WHOLE-D" THAT SANDWICH • • • • • • •

  Write a mixed number or a whole number for each picture.

**1.**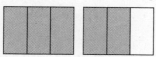

**2.**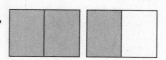

**3.** 

**4.** 

_____

_____

 Rename each fraction as a mixed or a whole number.

**5.** $\frac{5}{4}$          **6.** $\frac{9}{5}$          **7.** $\frac{10}{6}$          **8.** $\frac{15}{5}$

_____     _____     _____     _____

Rename each mixed number as a fraction.

**9.** $4\frac{3}{8}$          **10.** $3\frac{1}{2}$          **11.** $2\frac{1}{3}$          **12.** $9\frac{3}{4}$

_____     _____     _____     _____

 Arrange in order from least to greatest.

**13.** $3\frac{1}{4}$ , $3\frac{7}{8}$ , $3\frac{1}{3}$          **14.** $2\frac{1}{9}$ , $2\frac{3}{5}$ , $4\frac{1}{9}$

_____          _____

## Real World Connection

**Solve.**

**15.** Mido makes 6 sandwiches and cuts them in
half. He and his friends eat $4\frac{1}{2}$ sandwiches.
Draw a picture to show how many of the
sandwiches Mido and his friends eat.

**Fractions: Mixed Numbers**

Math 5, SV 8049-9

Name _____  Date _____

# • • • • • • • READING UP ON FRACTIONS • • • • • • •

 Write an addition or subtraction sentence for each drawing.

1.

_____

2.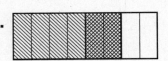

_____

 Find the sum or difference. Write the answer in simplest form.

3. $\dfrac{4}{8}$
$+\dfrac{3}{8}$

4. $\dfrac{3}{6}$
$+\dfrac{1}{6}$

5. $\dfrac{6}{8}$
$+\dfrac{1}{8}$

6. $\dfrac{7}{10}$
$-\dfrac{2}{10}$

7. $\dfrac{2}{4}$
$+\dfrac{1}{4}$

8. $\dfrac{4}{6}$
$-\dfrac{1}{6}$

9. $\dfrac{3}{5}$
$-\dfrac{1}{5}$

10. $\dfrac{9}{10}$
$-\dfrac{1}{10}$

11. $\dfrac{3}{6}$
$+\dfrac{2}{6}$

12. $\dfrac{5}{8}$
$-\dfrac{1}{8}$

13. $\dfrac{3}{8} + \dfrac{5}{8} =$ _____

14. $\dfrac{5}{9} - \dfrac{2}{9} =$ _____

15. $\dfrac{2}{7} + \dfrac{1}{7} =$ _____

16. $1 - \dfrac{2}{3} =$ _____

## Real World Connection

**Write the number sentence and solve.**

17. Pablo read for $\dfrac{5}{12}$ of an hour on Monday and $\dfrac{7}{12}$ of an hour on Tuesday. How many hours did he read during these two days?

_____

# ·········· PICTURE THESE FRACTIONS ········

**Tell whether one number is a multiple of the other. Write _yes_ or _no_.**

**1.** 6, 12 _____      **2.** 13, 26 _____      **3.** 8, 17 _____

$\frac{3}{8}$  $\frac{1}{4}$

**4.** 4, 9 _____      **5.** 6, 42 _____      **6.** 5, 8 _____

**Tell whether one denominator is a multiple of the other. Write _yes_ or _no_.**

**7.** $\frac{1}{5}, \frac{2}{10}$ _____   **8.** $\frac{3}{5}, \frac{1}{10}$ _____   **9.** $\frac{3}{4}, \frac{1}{5}$ _____   **10.** $\frac{2}{3}, \frac{3}{5}$ _____

**11.** $\frac{5}{10}, \frac{2}{5}$ _____   **12.** $\frac{3}{9}, \frac{5}{18}$ _____   **13.** $\frac{1}{12}, \frac{1}{5}$ _____   **14.** $\frac{5}{6}, \frac{7}{8}$ _____

**Rename the fractions to show the least common denominator.**

**15.** $\frac{1}{3}, \frac{1}{6} =$ _____      **16.** $\frac{5}{6}, \frac{1}{3} =$ _____      **17.** $\frac{7}{8}, \frac{3}{4} =$ _____

**18.** $\frac{9}{10}, \frac{1}{5} =$ _____      **19.** $\frac{2}{9}, \frac{1}{3} =$ _____      **20.** $\frac{3}{6}, \frac{1}{3} =$ _____

**21.** $\frac{1}{4}, \frac{2}{7} =$ _____      **22.** $\frac{3}{6}, \frac{1}{5} =$ _____      **23.** $\frac{2}{6}, \frac{1}{3} =$ _____

## Real World Connection

**Solve.**

**24.** There are 60 minutes in an hour. If Sandy takes 15 minutes to draw a picture, what part of an hour does he take?

_____

Name _____  Date _____

# ·········· SEWING UP FRACTIONS ··········

| Add or subtract. Write the answer in simplest form. |

1.  $\dfrac{1}{3}$
   $+\dfrac{1}{5}$

2.  $\dfrac{1}{2}$
   $+\dfrac{1}{5}$

3.  $\dfrac{4}{5}$
   $-\dfrac{1}{4}$

4.  $\dfrac{2}{3}$
   $+\dfrac{1}{6}$

5.  $\dfrac{7}{8}$
   $-\dfrac{1}{2}$

6.  $\dfrac{1}{2}$
   $-\dfrac{1}{4}$

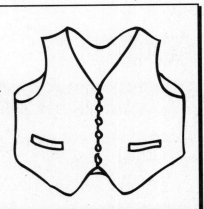

7.  $\dfrac{7}{10}$
   $-\dfrac{2}{5}$

8.  $\dfrac{1}{5}$
   $+\dfrac{1}{4}$

9.  $\dfrac{1}{6}$
   $+\dfrac{1}{2}$

10.  $\dfrac{1}{4}$
    $-\dfrac{1}{5}$

11. $\dfrac{2}{3} + \dfrac{1}{5} =$ _____

12. $\dfrac{7}{8} - \dfrac{1}{4} =$ _____

13. $\dfrac{3}{7} + \dfrac{1}{2} =$ _____

14. $\dfrac{1}{8} + \dfrac{1}{4} =$ _____

15. $\dfrac{1}{4} + \dfrac{5}{12} =$ _____

16. $\dfrac{2}{3} - \dfrac{1}{6} =$ _____

17. $\dfrac{2}{5} - \dfrac{3}{10} =$ _____

18. $\dfrac{5}{6} + \dfrac{1}{3} =$ _____

19. $\dfrac{3}{4} - \dfrac{1}{2} =$ _____

## Real World Connection

**Write the number sentence and solve.**

**20.** The dressmaker has $\dfrac{3}{8}$ yard of fabric. She needs a total of $\dfrac{3}{4}$ yard for a vest. How much more fabric does she need?

_____

Name _____   Date _____

# ·········· RAKING UP FRACTIONS ··········

Find the sum or difference. Write the answer in simplest form.

1.  $4\frac{3}{4}$
    $+ 2\frac{1}{8}$

2.  $2\frac{1}{3}$
    $- 1\frac{2}{3}$

3.  $6\frac{3}{8}$
    $+ 1\frac{1}{4}$

4.  $4\frac{1}{4}$
    $- 2\frac{3}{4}$

5.  $3\frac{4}{9}$
    $- 1\frac{8}{9}$

6.  $2\frac{1}{4}$
    $+ 2\frac{3}{4}$

7.  $3\frac{3}{5}$
    $- \frac{4}{5}$

8.  $6\frac{1}{4}$
    $+ 2\frac{1}{8}$

9.  $5\frac{1}{3}$
    $+ 1\frac{1}{6}$

10. $8$
    $- 3\frac{1}{8}$

11. $3\frac{3}{4}$
    $+ 1\frac{1}{8}$

12. $5\frac{6}{11}$
    $- 2\frac{9}{11}$

13. $3\frac{3}{4}$
    $+ 2\frac{3}{4}$

14. $3\frac{7}{8}$
    $+ 2\frac{1}{8}$

15. $7\frac{1}{5}$
    $- 3\frac{4}{5}$

16. $6\frac{1}{3}$
    $- 1\frac{2}{3}$

## Real World Connection

**Write the number sentence and solve.**

17. Susan raked $2\frac{3}{4}$ bags of leaves. Jay raked $2\frac{1}{4}$ bags of leaves. How many bags of leaves did they rake in all?

_____

# •••••••••• BUILDING FRACTIONS ••••••••••

| Add or subtract. Write the answer in simplest form. |

**1.** $9\frac{1}{6}$
$-8\frac{2}{3}$

**2.** $9\frac{4}{5}$
$+2\frac{3}{10}$

**3.** $8\frac{5}{9}$
$+6\frac{2}{3}$

**4.** $5\frac{1}{3}$
$-3\frac{4}{9}$

**5.** $7\frac{4}{5}$
$+8\frac{7}{20}$

**6.** $5\frac{1}{4}$
$-2\frac{11}{12}$

**7.** $8\frac{5}{6}$
$+3\frac{1}{3}$

**8.** $2\frac{1}{4}$
$-1\frac{5}{8}$

**9.** $8\frac{6}{7}$
$-2\frac{13}{14}$

**10.** $5\frac{2}{3}$
$+3\frac{5}{6}$

**11.** $4\frac{2}{3}$
$-2\frac{3}{4}$

**12.** $6\frac{1}{6}$
$+1\frac{11}{12}$

**13.** $5\frac{3}{8}$
$+2\frac{3}{4}$

**14.** $9\frac{1}{9}$
$-4\frac{2}{3}$

**15.** $5\frac{3}{4} + 6\frac{1}{12} = $ _____

**16.** $8\frac{1}{2} - 4\frac{7}{8} = $ _____

**17.** $5\frac{2}{3} + 4\frac{1}{3} = $ _____

**18.** $2\frac{1}{3} - 1\frac{1}{12} = $ _____

**19.** $12\frac{1}{16} + 4\frac{1}{4} = $ _____

**20.** $8\frac{7}{8} - 5\frac{1}{2} = $ _____

## Real World Connection

**Write the number sentence and solve.**

**21.** Joe has a piece of wood $15\frac{5}{6}$ ft long. He needs $11\frac{2}{3}$ ft for a project. How much wood will he have left?

_____

Name _____    Date _____

 ·········· **BAND "FUN" RAISING** ···········

 Write a number sentence for each picture.

**1.**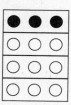

_____

**2.**

_____

**3.**

_____

**4.**

_____

 Multiply. Write the product as a mixed or whole number.

**5.** $\frac{1}{3} \times 15 =$ ____    **6.** $\frac{1}{4} \times 32 =$ ____    **7.** $\frac{3}{5} \times 15 =$ ____    **8.** $\frac{3}{4} \times 12 =$ ____

**9.** $\frac{1}{5} \times 20 =$ ____    **10.** $\frac{1}{3} \times 7 =$ ____    **11.** $\frac{4}{5} \times 2 =$ ____    **12.** $\frac{1}{3} \times 21 =$ ____

**13.** $\frac{5}{8} \times 10 =$ ____    **14.** $12 \times \frac{1}{3} =$ ____    **15.** $\frac{3}{5} \times 8 =$ ____    **16.** $\frac{3}{4} \times 3 =$ ____

## Real World Connection

**Write the number sentence and solve.**

**17.** The band has to sell 500 boxes of gourmet popcorn to raise funds for a trip. They have sold $\frac{3}{5}$ of the boxes. How many more boxes do they have to sell?

_____

Name _____     Date _____

 Write a number sentence for each drawing.

**1.**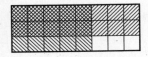

**2.**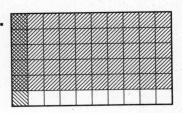

_____        _____

Multiply. Write the answer in simplest form.

**3.** $\frac{3}{4} \times \frac{1}{2} =$ _____

**4.** $\frac{2}{3} \times \frac{1}{9} =$ _____

**5.** $\frac{2}{5} \times \frac{1}{5} =$ _____

**6.** $\frac{1}{5} \times \frac{1}{2} =$ _____

**7.** $\frac{2}{17} \times \frac{1}{4} =$ _____

**8.** $\frac{5}{12} \times \frac{1}{5} =$ _____

**9.** $\frac{1}{3} \times \frac{1}{9} =$ _____

**10.** $\frac{3}{10} \times \frac{3}{10} =$ _____

**11.** $\frac{1}{3} \times \frac{5}{12} =$ _____

**12.** $\frac{2}{3} \times \frac{2}{9} =$ _____

**13.** $\frac{1}{4} \times \frac{3}{4} =$ _____

**14.** $\frac{5}{7} \times \frac{1}{5} =$ _____

**15.** $\frac{4}{5} \times \frac{1}{3} =$ _____

**16.** $\frac{3}{7} \times \frac{1}{2} =$ _____

**17.** $\frac{1}{2} \times \frac{5}{8} =$ _____

## Real World Connection

**Write the number sentence and solve.**

**18.** Joan has $\frac{3}{4}$ yd of fabric. She needs $\frac{2}{3}$ of that amount to make a small flag. How much fabric will she need in all?

_____

Name _____ Date _____

# ···AN "EGG-STRA" DOZEN OF FRACTIONS···

Write a number sentence for each picture.

**1.**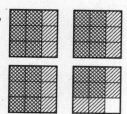

_____

**2.**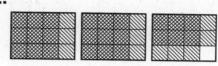

_____

Draw fraction squares to help you find each product.

**3.** $\frac{1}{3} \times 2\frac{2}{3} =$ _____

**4.** $\frac{3}{4} \times 2\frac{1}{4} =$ _____

**5.** $\frac{1}{2} \times 2\frac{1}{8} =$ _____

**6.** $\frac{3}{4} \times 3\frac{1}{2} =$ _____

**7.** $\frac{2}{3} \times 1\frac{1}{2} =$ _____

**8.** $\frac{5}{8} \times 1\frac{1}{2} =$ _____

**9.** $\frac{2}{5} \times 1\frac{1}{2} =$ _____

**10.** $\frac{4}{7} \times 2\frac{2}{3} =$ _____

**11.** $\frac{1}{4} \times 3\frac{1}{7} =$ _____

## Real World Connection

**Write the number sentence and solve.**

**12.** The chickens laid $6\frac{1}{4}$ dozen eggs. The farmer sold $\frac{2}{5}$ of them. How many eggs did the farmer sell?

_____

Name _____ Date _____

# ···· A RECIPE FOR DIVIDING FRACTIONS ····

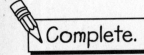 **Complete.**

1. How many fives are in twenty-five? _____

2. How many fours are in twelve? _____

3. How many threes are in twelve? _____

**Write a division number sentence for each picture.**

4.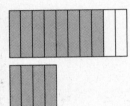

5.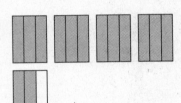

6.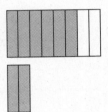

_____  _____  _____

**Use the rule for dividing fractions with like denominators.**

7. $\frac{2}{3} \div \frac{1}{3} =$ _____

8. $\frac{4}{5} \div \frac{2}{5} =$ _____

9. $\frac{12}{15} \div \frac{4}{15} =$ _____

10. $\frac{8}{9} \div \frac{4}{9} =$ _____

11. $\frac{6}{7} \div \frac{2}{7} =$ _____

12. $\frac{3}{4} \div \frac{3}{4} =$ _____

13. $\frac{9}{11} \div \frac{3}{11} =$ _____

14. $\frac{2}{9} \div \frac{2}{9} =$ _____

15. $\frac{9}{14} \div \frac{3}{14} =$ _____

16. $\frac{8}{15} \div \frac{2}{15} =$ _____

17. $\frac{3}{5} \div \frac{1}{5} =$ _____

18. $\frac{10}{16} \div \frac{2}{16} =$ _____

## Real World Connection

**Write the number sentence and solve.**

19. Joan is making valentines. She has $\frac{2}{3}$ sheet of paper. Each valentine takes $\frac{1}{6}$ sheet. How many valentines can Joan make?

_____

Name _____  Date _____

# ·········· "WEATHER" OR NOT ··········

Solve. Write each answer in simplest form.

1. $\frac{4}{6}$
   $+ \frac{1}{6}$

2. $\frac{4}{5}$
   $- \frac{1}{5}$

3. $\frac{2}{3}$
   $\times \frac{3}{4}$

4. $\frac{4}{5}$
   $+ \frac{2}{10}$ _____

5. $5\frac{7}{9}$
   $- \frac{8}{9}$

6. $3\frac{1}{4}$
   $+ 1\frac{3}{8}$

7. $2\frac{3}{5}$
   $- 1\frac{1}{3}$

8. $32$
   $\times \frac{1}{4}$

9. $6\frac{1}{2}$
   $+ 2\frac{3}{4}$

10. $10\frac{1}{4}$
    $- 2\frac{3}{4}$

11. $5\frac{4}{5}$
    $- 1\frac{1}{4}$

12. $4\frac{3}{4}$
    $+ 2\frac{1}{4}$

13. $\frac{1}{3}$
    $\times \frac{3}{4}$

14. $\frac{5}{8} \times 1\frac{1}{2} =$ _____

15. $\frac{4}{5} \div \frac{2}{5} =$ _____

16. $6\frac{1}{6} + 1\frac{11}{12} =$ _____

17. $\frac{3}{5} \div \frac{2}{5} =$ _____

18. $\frac{3}{4} \times \frac{1}{2} =$ _____

19. $8\frac{6}{7} - 2\frac{13}{14} =$ _____

20. $6\frac{1}{2} + 3\frac{3}{4} =$ _____

21. $6 - 4\frac{1}{4} =$ _____

22. $4 \div \frac{2}{3} =$ _____

## Real World Connection

**Write the number sentence and solve.**

23. In January, Bolton received $2\frac{3}{4}$ inches of rain. In February the town received $1\frac{2}{3}$ inches of rain. What was the total rainfall for January and February?

_____

**Fractions: Mixed Practice**

Math 5, SV 8049-9

# ···· REPORTS ABOUT PROBLEM SOLVING ····

Choose the strategy and solve.

**1.** Chen's report will take $8\frac{1}{3}$ hours to complete. He has worked for $\frac{3}{5}$ of that time doing research. How long has he worked?

_____

**2.** Suki worked for $3\frac{3}{4}$ hours on her report on Monday and $6\frac{1}{2}$ hours on Tuesday. How many hours did she work in all?

_____

**3.** Of the 36 students in the class, $\frac{5}{6}$ want to do an oral report as a presentation. How many want to give a different kind of presentation?

_____

**4.** There are 60 minutes in an hour. If Sandy takes 15 minutes to give her oral report, what part of an hour does she take?

_____

**5.** Jose's written report is $12\frac{1}{2}$ pages long. Marian's report is $9\frac{1}{3}$ pages long. How much longer is Jose's report?

_____

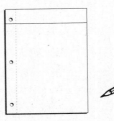

# ······ GOING TO THE METRIC LENGTHS ······

Circle **a**, **b**, or **c** to tell which measurement is the most reasonable.

1.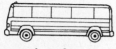

   length of a bus

   **a.** 12 km    **b.** 12 m    **c.** 12 cm

2.

   height of a television

   **a.** 4 cm    **b.** 4 km    **c.** 4 dm

3.

   diameter of a baseball

   **a.** 7 cm    **b.** 7 m    **c.** 7 km

Write the measure to the nearest cm and then write a more precise measure.

4. _____

_____

5. _____

_____

6. _____

_____

## Real World Connection

**Write the number sentence and solve.**

7. A vine grew 6 cm the first week, 4.3 cm the second week, 5.1 cm the third week, and 7.8 cm the fourth week. How many cm is that?

_____

Measurement: Metric Lengths

Math 5, SV 8049-9

Name _____     Date _____

# •••••••••••• FILL IT FULL ••••••••••••

## Choose the more reasonable estimate of capacity. Circle **a** or **b**.

**1.** cup of tea

**a.** 250 mL
**b.** 250 L

**2.** paint bucket

**a.** 2 mL
**b.** 2 L

**3.** contact lens case

**a.** 40 mL
**b.** 40 L

**4.** bath tub

**a.** 450 mL
**b.** 450 L

## Choose the more reasonable unit of measure. Write **mL** or **L**.

**5.** fish tank

_____

**6.** glass

_____

**7.** large pot

_____

**8.** trash barrel

_____

**9.** thimble

_____

**10.** swimming pool

_____

## Complete.

**11.** 2.091 L = 2,091 _____

**12.** 16,000 mL = 16 _____

**13.** 50.5 mL = _____ L

**14.** 406.2 L = _____ mL

## Real World Connection

**Solve.**

**15.** Kyle is making lemonade from a powdered mix. The container says one scoop of powder will make 0.75 L. How many scoops are needed to make 3 L?

_____

Name _____     Date _____

# •••••••••••• "WEIGHT" FOR ME ••••••••••••

 Choose the most reasonable unit. Write **kg**, **g**, or **mg**.

**1.** a computer

_____

**2.** a dime

_____

**3.** a calculator

_____

**4.** a basket of apples

_____

Choose the more reasonable estimate of mass. Circle **a** or **b**.

**5.**      **a.** 1 kg
             **b.** 1 g

**6.**      **a.** 8 kg
             **b.** 8 g

For Exercises 7–10, write how many portions can be made.

Raisins
120 g

COCONUT
1,500 mg

Cereal
850 g

**7.** 50-g portions of cereal

_____

**8.** 15-g portions of raisins

_____

**9.** 5-g portions of raisins

_____

**10.** 75-mg portions of coconut

_____

## Real World Connection

**Write the number sentence and solve.**

**11.** Three blueberry muffins have a mass of 65 grams. What is the mass of 3 dozen blueberry muffins?

_____

# • • • • • • • THE TALL AND SHORT OF IT • • • • • • •

Measure each line segment to the part of the inch that gives the *most* precise measurement.

1. _____   _____

2. _____   _____

3. _____   _____

4. _____   _____

Draw a line to the given length.

5. $1\frac{1}{2}$ in.

6. $2\frac{1}{8}$ in.

7. $3\frac{1}{4}$ in.

8. $\frac{9}{16}$ in.

Complete.

9. 2 ft = _____ in.

10. 1.5 mi = _____ yd

11. 50 yd = _____ ft

12. 24 in. = _____ ft

13. 2,640 ft = _____ yd

14. 12 ft = _____ yd

15. 5,280 yd = _____ mi

16. 108 in. = _____ yd

17. 15,840 ft = _____ mi

## Real World Connection

**Write the number sentence and solve.**

18. Bayard is 5 ft 5 $\frac{3}{4}$ in. tall. José is 5 ft 5 $\frac{9}{16}$ in. tall. Who is taller? How much taller is he?

_____

# • • • • • • • GIVE IT ANOTHER NAME • • • • • • •

POUNDS

### Write *multiply* or *divide*.

**1.** to change pounds to ounces

**2.** to change pounds to tons

_____

_____

**3.** to change pints to cups

**4.** to change quarts to gallons

_____

_____

**5.** to change ounces to cups

**6.** to change quarts to pints

_____

_____

### Complete.

**7.** 24 qt = _____ gal

**8.** 12 qt = _____ c

**9.** 7 pt = _____ c

**10.** 4 c = _____ fl oz

**11.** 24 pt = _____ q

**12.** $2\frac{3}{4}$ gal = _____ qt

**13.** 4 gal = _____ qt

**14.** 3 gal = _____ pt

**15.** 8 qt = _____ pt

**16.** 512 oz = _____ lb

**17.** 128 oz = _____ lb

**18.** 48 oz = _____ lb

**19.** $4\frac{1}{4}$ lb = _____ oz

**20.** 5,000 lb = _____ T

**21.** $6\frac{1}{2}$ T = _____ lb

## Real World Connection

**Write the number sentence and solve.**

**22.** Ella's doctor told her she should drink 2.5 gal of water every week during the summer. How many 8-oz glasses of water should she drink in a week?

_____

Name _____ Date _____

# ••••••••••••• TIME CHANGE •••••••••••••

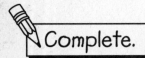 Complete.

**1.** 4 yr = _____ mo

**2.** 7 days = _____ hr

**3.** 108 mo = _____ yr

**4.** 10 min = _____ sec     **5.** 3 wk = _____ days

**6.** 2 yr = _____ days     **7.** 72 hr = _____ days

**8.** 6 hr = _____ min     **9.** 91 days = _____ wk

**10.** 210 hr = _____ days _____ hr     **11.** 3 hr 22 min = _____ min

**12.** 411 wk = _____ yr _____ wk     **13.** 511 d = _____ yr _____ days

**14.** 62 mo = _____ yr _____ mo     **15.** 1,024 sec = _____ min _____ sec

**16.** 2 yr = _____ hr     **17.** 3,648 sec = _____ hr _____ sec

**18.** 208 wk = _____ yr     **19.** 1 wk = _____ sec

## Real World Connection

**Write the number sentence and solve.**

**20.** Anita volunteers at the school library for 3 hours each day. How many hours does she volunteer in a 180-day school year?

_____

Name _____  Date _____

# • • • • • • • • • • • WATCH THE TIME • • • • • • • • • • •

## Compute the time when each event began or ended.

1. Leslie arrived at school at 7:25 A.M. It takes Leslie 45 min to walk to school.

_____

2. Lunch is served at 12:30 P.M. It takes 52 min to prepare lunch.

_____

3. Dinner is served at 6:00 P.M. It takes 17 min to eat dinner.

_____

4. A boat arrived on Tuesday at 6:15 A.M. The boat was on the ocean for 4 days, 2 hr, and 34 min.

_____

## Add or subtract.

5.　  6 hr 21 min
　  − 3 hr 53 min

6.　  4 min 25 sec
　  + 5 min 51 sec

7.　  8 min 19 sec
　  − 4 min 46 sec

8.　  6 hr 20 min
　  + 2 hr 43 min

9.　  8 min 15 sec
　  − 7 min 31 sec

10.　  8 hr  0 min
　  − 4 hr 34 min

## Real World Connection

**Solve.**

11. Kevin started his homework at 6:50 P.M. He took a 30-min break and finished his work at 9:15 P.M. How long did he work on his homework?

Name _____    Date _____

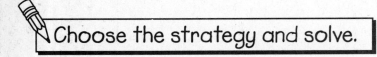

Choose the strategy and solve.

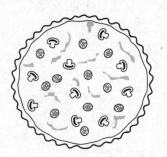

1. Rizzo's Pizzeria makes a large pizza that weighs 5 pounds. The crust and sauce weigh 2 pounds 3 ounces. How much do the toppings weigh?

_____

2. Mr. Rizzo takes a pizza out of the oven at 7:10. The pizza took 15 minutes to make and 20 minutes to bake. At what time did Mr. Rizzo start to make the pizza?

_____

3. When Mr. Rizzo makes pizza sauce, he uses 2 cans of tomato sauce that weigh 822 grams each and 1 can of tomato paste that weighs 340 grams. He makes 16 pizzas from this recipe. How many grams of sauce does he put on each pizza?

_____

4. Rizzo's Pizzeria sells 1 gallon of lemonade for $2.09, a quart of lemonade for $0.79, and 1 pint of lemonade for $0.25. Which is the best way to buy 1 gal of lemonade?

_____

5. Ben delivers pizza for Rizzo's Pizzeria. He drives 13.7 kilometers to make a delivery at one house and then another 3.8 kilometers to make the second delivery. Ben drives 8.2 kilometers to get back to the restaurant. How many kilometers did Ben drive in all?

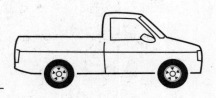

_____

# •••••••••• ON THE LINE ••••••••••

Choose the sentence that describes the relationship of the lines. Circle **a**, **b**, or **c**.

**1.**

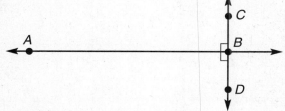

  **a.** $\overleftrightarrow{AB}$ is parallel to $\overleftrightarrow{CD}$.

  **b.** $\overleftrightarrow{AB}$ is perpendicular to $\overleftrightarrow{CD}$.

  **c.** $\overleftrightarrow{AB}$ is not perpendicular to $\overleftrightarrow{CD}$.

**2.**

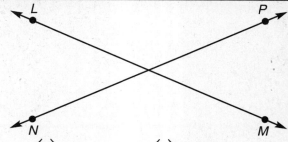

  **a.** $\overleftrightarrow{LM}$ intersects $\overleftrightarrow{NP}$.

  **b.** $\overleftrightarrow{LM}$ is perpendicular to $\overleftrightarrow{NP}$.

  **c.** $\overleftrightarrow{LM}$ is parallel to $\overleftrightarrow{NP}$.

**3.**

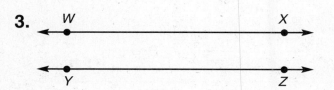

  **a.** $\overleftrightarrow{WX}$ intersects $\overleftrightarrow{YZ}$.

  **b.** $\overleftrightarrow{WX}$ is parallel to $\overleftrightarrow{YZ}$.

  **c.** $\overleftrightarrow{WX}$ is perpendicular to $\overleftrightarrow{YZ}$.

**4.**

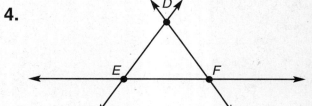

  **a.** $\overleftrightarrow{DE}$ intersects $\overleftrightarrow{EF}$.

  **b.** $\overleftrightarrow{DE}$ is perpendicular to $\overleftrightarrow{EF}$.

  **c.** $\overleftrightarrow{EF}$ is parallel to $\overleftrightarrow{DF}$.

## Real World Connection

**Solve.**

  **5.** The map shows the downtown area of Cantorville. Which street runs parallel to Courthouse Road?

_____

Name _____     Date _____

 • • • • • • • • • • • **ANGLE OF THE RAYS** • • • • • • • • • • • •

**Identify the angle. Write _right_, _acute_, or _obtuse_.**

**1.** _____    **2.** _____    **3.** _____

**Use a protractor to measure each angle.**

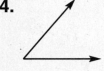

**4.** Measure _____    **5.** Measure _____

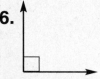

**6.** Measure _____    **7.** Measure _____

**Use a protractor to draw an angle with the given measure.**

**8.** 45°          **9.** 90°          **10.** 120°

**11.** 25°         **12.** 75°         **13.** 145°

## Real World Connection

**Solve.**

**14.** Draw hands on the clock to show 4:15. What kind of angle is formed by the hands of the clock?

_____

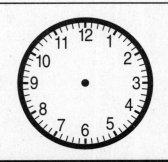

Name _____    Date _____

# SIGNING WITH SHAPES

## Name a polygon represented by each object.

**1.** flag          **2.** football field          **3.**           **4.**

_____    _____    _____    _____

**5.** Circle the regular polygons.

## Draw and name the quadrilateral.

**6.** opposite sides are parallel and the same length; no right angles

**7.** four sides of equal length; four right angles

**8.** four sides of equal length; opposite sides are parallel; no right angles

**9.** one pair of parallel sides

## Real World Connection

**Solve.**

**10.** Manny cut a figure out of paper to make a sign. He called it a rectangle. His teacher called it a square. Could they both be correct? Explain.

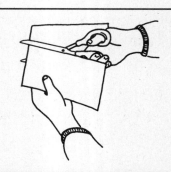

_____

# • • • • PLAYING AROUND WITH TRIANGLES • • • •

 Name each triangle. Write **equilateral**, **scalene**, or **isosceles**.

**1.**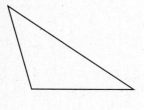

_____

**2.**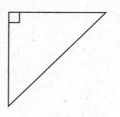

_____

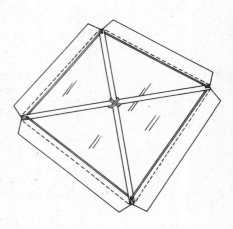

**3.**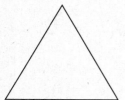

_____

**4.**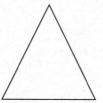

_____

 Name each triangle. Write **right**, **acute**, or **obtuse**.

**5.**

_____

**6.**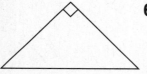

_____

**7.**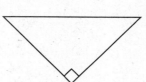

_____

**8.**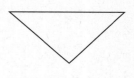

_____

## Real World Connection

**Solve.**

**9.** The playground at Molly's school is in the shape of an equilateral triangle. The playground at David's school is in the shape of an acute triangle. Could Molly and David go to the same school? Explain.

_____

# •••••••••• SWIMMING IN CIRCLES ••••••••••

 **Write *sometimes*, *always*, or *never*.**

1. A radius _____ connects two points on a circle.

2. A diameter _____ passes through the center of the circle.

3. A radius _____ connects the center of the circle with a point on the circle.

4. A chord _____ passes through the center of the circle.

 **Use the drawing for Exercises 5–7.**

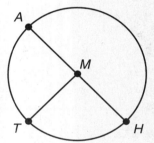

5. Name the center of this circle. _____

6. Name a radius. _____

7. Name a diameter. _____

**Complete. Use the drawing for Exercises 8–11.**

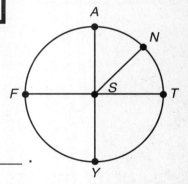

8. Line segment *FT* is a _____ .

9. The center of the circle is _____ .

10. Line segment *AS* is a _____ .

11. Points *A* and *Y* are endpoints of a _____ .

## Real World Connection

**Solve.**

12. Sid's circular pool has a radius of 8 ft. What is the longest distance a swimmer can swim without making a turn?

_____

• • • • • • • • • • • • • • **MATCHED UP** • • • • • • • • • • • • • • •

 Tell which figures can be folded on the dotted line to show a mirror image. Write **yes** or **no**.

1.

_____

2.

_____

3.

_____

4.

_____

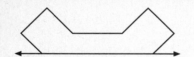 Draw all the lines of symmetry for each figure.

5.      6.      7.

Complete the design to make a symmetrical figure.

8. 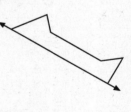     9.      10.

## Real World Connection

**Use the list of letters to solve Exercises 11-12.**

# A B C D E F G H I J K L M

11. Which letters have no lines of symmetry?

12. Which letters have only one line of symmetry?

# • • • • • • • • • • FIGURES IN MOTION • • • • • • • • • •

 **Follow the directions.**

**1.** Flip the figure across the line.

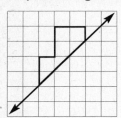

**2.** Turn the rectangle around vertex A until it sits on another side.

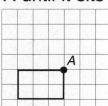

 Write **slide**, **flip**, or **turn** to indicate how each figure was moved.

**3.**

_____

**4.**

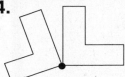

_____

**5.**

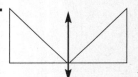

_____

Are the figures similar? Write **yes** or **no**.

**6.** _____

**7.** _____

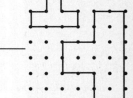

**8.** _____

Draw a larger figure that is similar.

**9.**

## Real World Connection

**Solve.**

**10.** Name the motion made by the seats on a Ferris wheel.

_____

Name _____   Date _____

 Name the solid. Then write the number of vertices (**V**), edges (**E**), and faces (**F**).

1.   V _____
              E _____
_____  F _____

2.   V _____
              E _____
_____  F _____

3.  V _____
              E _____
_____  F _____

4.  V _____
              E _____
_____  F _____

5.   V _____
              E _____
_____  F _____

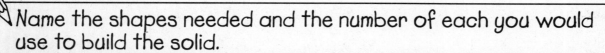 Name the shapes needed and the number of each you would use to build the solid.

6. cylinder

_____

7. square pyramid

_____

8. rectangular prism

_____

## Real World Connection

**Solve.**

9. Janna has four congruent triangles and a square. What solid figure can she make?

_____

Name _____  Date _____

 ······· *PUZZLED ABOUT PERIMETERS* ·······

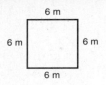 Find the perimeter of each figure.

**1.**
6 m
6 m    6 m
6 m

_____

**2.**
6 mm    10 mm
8 mm

_____

**3.**
7 m

_____

**4.**
15 ft
9 ft    11 ft
22 ft

_____

**5.**
7 cm
13 cm

_____

**6.**
7 ft

_____

**7.**
12 m
14 m    9 m
15 m

_____

**8.**
7 ft    4 ft
8 ft
9 ft
8 ft

_____

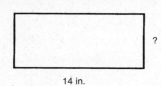 Find the missing length in each figure.

**9.**
?
14 in.

Perimeter = 42 in.

_____

**10.**
?
27 yd    27 yd
35 yd

Perimeter = 119 yd

_____

**11.**
?

Perimeter = 28 ft

_____

## Real World Connection

**Solve.**

**12.** Steve is working on a jigsaw puzzle. When it is finished, he would like to frame it. If the puzzle measures 14 in. x 16 in., how many inches of frame will Steve need?

_____

# • • • • • • • • • MEASURE AROUND • • • • • • • • •

 **Find the circumference. Round to the nearest tenth.**

**1.**

22.3 mm

_____

**2.**

15.5 mm

_____

**3.**

17.9 mm

_____

**4.**

28.5 mm

_____

 **Find the diameter. Round to the nearest tenth.**

**5.** C = 84.5 cm          **6.** C = 25.8 cm          **7.** C = 189.6 cm

_____          _____          _____

  **Find the circumference.**

**8.**  Diameter = 13.6 cm     Circumference = _____

**9.**  Diameter = 23.9 cm     Circumference = _____

## Real World Connection

**Write the number sentence and solve.**

**10.** The largest hamburger in the world was 5,005 lb 13.8 oz. It had a diameter of 23 ft 3 $\frac{1}{2}$ in. and was cut into 15,750 portions after grilling. Determine its circumference in inches.

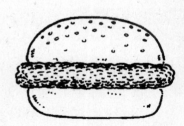

_____

# •••••••• MUSIC IS IN THE "AIR-EA" ••••••••

 Find each area. Each square equals 1 cm².

**1.**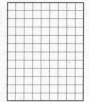

**2.**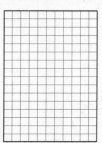

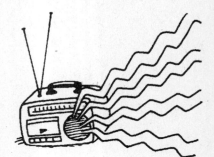

_____  _____

 Use the formula to find the area of each rectangle.

**3.**
9 in.    4 in.

**4.**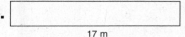
17 m    3 m

**5.**
13 in.    6 in.

_____  _____  _____

Measure each side to the nearest millimeter. Then find the area.

**6.**

**7.**

**8.**

_____  _____  _____

## Real World Connection

**Write the number sentence and solve.**

**9.** The music room at the elementary school is 25 ft long and 35 ft wide. What is the area of the room?

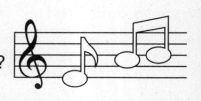

# PARKING AREA

## Find the area of each figure.

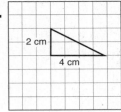

**1.**

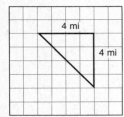

4 cm

3 cm

_____

**2.**

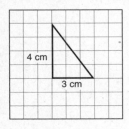

4 cm

2 cm

_____

**3.**

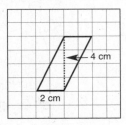

4 mi

4 mi

_____

**4.**

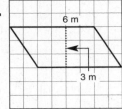

6 m

3 m

_____

**5.**

2 cm

4 cm

_____

**6.** parallelogram

$b = 7$ in.

$h = 9$ in.

_____

**7.** triangle

$b = 12$ m

$h = 8$ m

_____

**8.** parallelogram

$b = 5$ ft

$h = 17$ ft

_____

**9.** triangle

$b = 7$ ft

$h = 4$ ft

_____

**10.** parallelogram

$b = 3$ ft

$h = 7$ ft

_____

**11.** triangle

$b = 9$ in.

$h = 8$ in.

_____

## Real World Connection

**Write the number sentence and solve.**

**12.** A park is in the shape of a triangle with base 120 m
and height 48 m. What is the area of the park?

_____

·········· **IN YOUR BACKYARD** ··········

 Find the area of each complex figure.

**1.**
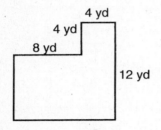
4 yd
4 yd
8 yd
12 yd

_____

**2.**
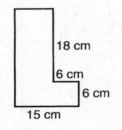
18 cm
6 cm
6 cm
15 cm

_____

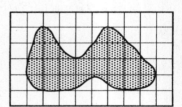

**3.**
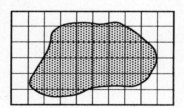
12 m
4 m
4 m    4 m
8 m

_____

**4.**
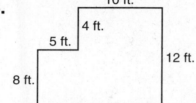
10 ft.
4 ft.
5 ft.
12 ft.
8 ft.

_____

Estimate the area of each curved figure. Each unit equals 1 mm².

**5.**
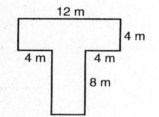

_____

**6.**

_____

## Real World Connection

**Solve.**

**7.** Joy's backyard measures 25 ft by 40 ft. Sofia's backyard measures 30 ft by 30 ft. Who has a bigger yard and by how much?

_____

# • • • • • • • • • • • • BUILDING BLOCKS • • • • • • • • • • • •

| Use what you know about hidden cubes to find the number of cubes used to build each figure. |

**1.**

_____

**2.**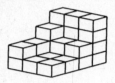

_____

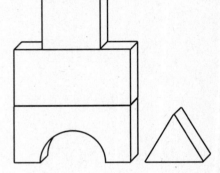

**3.**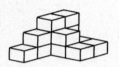

_____

**4.**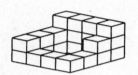

_____

**5.**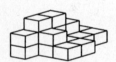

_____

**6.**

_____

**7.**

_____

**8.** For which of the figures above is this the top view?

**9.** Name three figures above for which this is a side view.

_____

## Real World Connection

**Solve.**

**10.** Mr. Kwong is putting math cubes back into boxes. He has 60 blocks left. Estimate the number of blocks that Mr. Kwong can put into the box. Will the 60 blocks fit?

_____

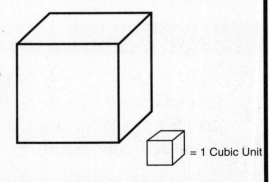

= 1 Cubic Unit

# • • • • • • • • • • • • • • • • BOXED IN • • • • • • • • • • • • • • • •

### Find the volume of each prism in cm³.

**1.**
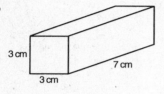

3 cm
3 cm
7 cm

_____

**2.**
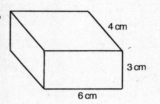

4 cm
3 cm
6 cm

_____

**3.**
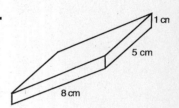

1 cm
5 cm
8 cm

_____

**4.**
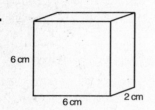

6 cm
6 cm
2 cm

_____

**5.**
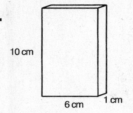

10 cm
6 cm
1 cm

_____

**6.**
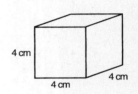

4 cm
4 cm
4 cm

_____

### Find the volume of each.

**7.**

75 ft × 25 ft × 8 ft

_____

**8.**

14 in. × 9 in. × 7 in.

_____

**9.** $l$ = 7 in.
$w$ = 8 in.
$h$ = 5 in.

_____

**10.** $l$ = 20 ft
$w$ = 10 ft
$h$ = 5 ft

_____

**11.** $l$ = 50 yd
$w$ = 25 yd
$h$ = 10 yd

_____

## Real World Connection

**Write the number sentence and solve.**

**12.** A dresser has 4 drawers. Each measures 5 dm by 4 dm by 2 dm. What is the maximum storage space available for the dresser?

_____

# ······· PROBLEM SOLVING ON STAGE ·······

| Choose the strategy and solve. |

**1.** To make the background scenery for a play, a picture is painted on a roll of paper that measures 12 ft by 8 ft. The painter needs to frame the back of it with wood so it will stand up. How many feet of wood does the painter need?

_____

**2.** The smallest spotlight on stage has a diameter of 30 in. What is the circumference?

_____

**3.** Lana builds the sets on stage. Her toolbox is 20 in. long, 12 in. wide, and 10 in. high. Find the volume of Lana's toolbox.

_____

**4.** Joel is designing a prop for the play. He draws a model first. Joel draws a circle on a piece of 1-cm graph paper. It covers 20 squares and 6 partial squares. Estimate the area of the circle.

_____

**5.** Shawn has four congruent triangles. He builds the last part of the scenery. What solid figure does he make?

_____

Name _____ Date _____

# • • • • • • • • • • • • • • • TRY A SAMPLE • • • • • • • • • • • • • •

| Choose a word or words from the box to complete each sentence. |

1. The _____ collected from a sample group can help you _____ the most frequent choice of a larger group.

2. To find the most frequent choice of a group, conduct a _____.

3. People with different interests have the same chance of being chosen when the group is chosen at _____.

| predict |
| random |
| survey |
| data |

4. Tell which sample group would better predict the most frequent choice of adults. Defend your answer.

| Hiking Club Sample Group Favorite Pastime | |
|---|---|
| **Pastime** | **Number of Adults** |
| Physical Activity | 26 |
| Television Viewing | 6 |
| Hobby | 8 |
| Other | 10 |

| Random Sample Group Favorite Pastime | |
|---|---|
| **Pastime** | **Number of Adults** |
| Physical Activity | 14 |
| Television Viewing | 8 |
| Hobby | 12 |
| Other | 16 |

_____     _____

_____     _____

## Real World Connection

**Solve.**

5. Take a survey of at least ten people to find their favorite pastime. Complete the frequency table from your data.

| Random Sample Group Favorite Pastimes | | |
|---|---|---|
| **Name** | **Tallies** | **Frequencies** |
| | | |
| | | |
| | | |
| | | |
| | | |

# ········ DO YOU GET THE PICTURE? ········

Use the pictograph about the election for Exercises 1–4.

| Result of Student Council Election | |
| --- | --- |
| **Person** | **Number of Votes** |
| Fran | □ □ □ □ □ □ □ □ ▷ |
| Ben | □ □ □ □ □ □ |
| Crissy | □ □ □ □ □ □ □ □ □ |
| Anil | □ □ □ □ □ □ |
| Angelina | □ □ □ □ ▷ |

□ = 10 votes

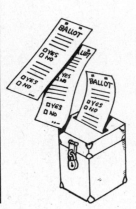

1. Which two students got the same number of votes?

   _____

2. Who got the most votes?

   _____

3. How many votes did Fran get?

   _____

4. What was the total number of votes for Angelina and Crissy?

## Real World Connection

**Solve.**

5. If the key in a pictograph has a symbol that represents 4 students, how many symbols would be needed to represent 50 students?

   _____

**Graphs: Pictographs**

Math 5, SV 8049-9

Name _____    Date _____

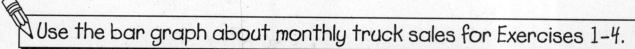

## GRAPHS WITH BARS

Use the bar graph about monthly truck sales for Exercises 1-4.

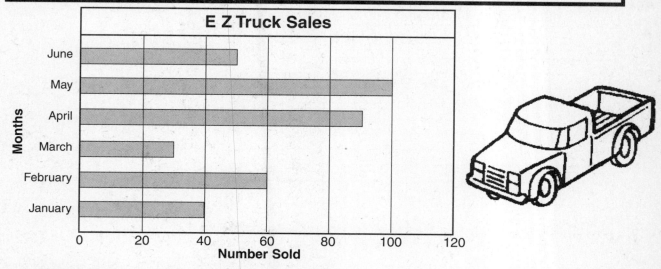

**E Z Truck Sales**

Months (June, May, April, March, February, January)

Number Sold: 0, 20, 40, 60, 80, 100, 120

1. What scale is shown on the graph?

   _____

2. Were more trucks sold in January or in March?

   _____

3. How many trucks were sold in June?

   _____

4. What is the month in which more than 70 but fewer than 100 trucks were sold?

   _____

## Real World Connection

**Solve.**

5. Make a table that shows the number of students in your class who participate in various sports. Use the data from the table to make a bar graph. Choose a scale, title and label your graph, and then color in the bars.

Name _____     Date _____

# ······· GRAPHING ALONG THE LINES ·······

Use the line graph for Exercises 1–4.

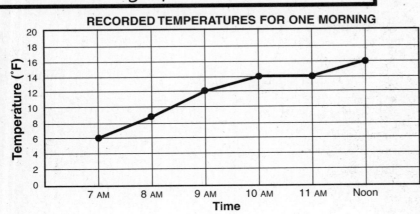

**RECORDED TEMPERATURES FOR ONE MORNING**

1. At what time was the highest temperature recorded?

   _____

2. At which two times was the same temperature recorded?

   _____

3. About what temperature was it at 8 A.M.?

   _____

4. Between which two hours was the greatest increase in temperature recorded?

   _____

## Real World Connection

**Solve.**

5. Make a line graph to show the data on the table.
   Choose a scale, title, and label your graph.

| Raffle Ticket Sales | |
|---|---|
| **Month** | **Number Sold** |
| July | 200 |
| August | 180 |
| September | 150 |
| October | 170 |
| November | 200 |

# •••••••••• AROUND A GRAPH ••••••••••

**Use the graph to answer the questions.**

**AFTER-SCHOOL ACTIVITIES OF 40 STUDENTS**

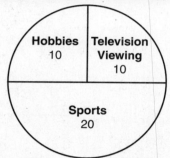

Hobbies 10 | Television Viewing 10 | Sports 20

1. What is the title of the graph?

   _____

2. How is each part of the graph labeled?

   _____

3. How does the part of the class that prefers television viewing compare to the part that prefers sports?

   _____

   _____

4. How would you change the graph if the same number of students liked each choice? Draw the new circle graph.

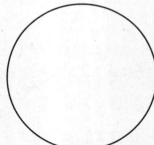

## Real World Connection

**Solve.**

5. Harry planted 27 bulbs in the fall. Of the bulbs he planted, $\frac{2}{3}$ bloomed in the spring, but $\frac{1}{3}$ did not bloom. Draw the circle graph. Show the number of bulbs represented by each part of the graph. Remember to give the graph a title.

# ·········· HOUSES MADE TO ORDER ··········

Use the grid and legend for Exercises 1–8. Name the coordinates of each location.

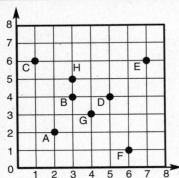

**Legend**
A Art's house
B Barbara's house
C Claire's house
D Denny's house
E Ellen's house
F Franco's house
G Gloria's house
H Hugo's house

**1.** Barbara's house _____

**2.** Franco's house _____

**3.** Gloria's house _____

**4.** Hugo's house _____

Name the person whose house is at each of the following coordinates.

**5.** (2,2) _____    **6.** (1,6) _____    **7.** (7,6) _____    **8.** (5,4) _____

**9.** Mark the points at coordinates (1,1),(1,3),(4,3), and (4,1). Connect the points in order. Then connect the first and last points. What figure did you make?

_____

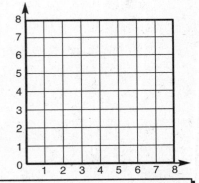

## Real World Connection

**Solve.**

**10.** On the grid, draw a simple house made up of line segments. Make a list of coordinates that must be connected to make the house. Give the list of coordinates to a partner. Have the partner use the coordinates to draw the house on another grid.

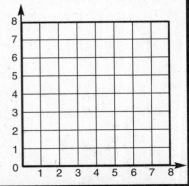

# ····· PROBLEM SOLVING IN PICTURES ······

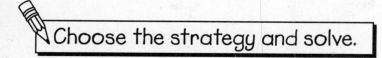

**Choose the strategy and solve.**

1. Soon-Li took a poll of favorite foods of fifth graders. She made a pictograph to show the data. Each pizza symbol represented 8 votes. She drew $9\frac{1}{2}$ symbols for hot dogs. How many people voted for hot dogs?

_____

2. Make a bar graph to show the data below.

**FAVORITE SPORTS**

| Sport | Number of Students |
|-------|--------------------|
| Baseball | 20 |
| Soccer | 30 |
| Tennis | 10 |
| Basketball | 15 |

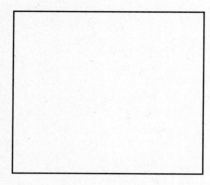

3. The table show the hours Wendy works. If the pattern continues, how many hours will she work in the ninth week? Show the data on a line graph. _____

**WENDY'S HOURS OF WORK**

| | |
|---|---|
| Week 1 | 12 hours |
| Week 2 | 14 hours |
| Week 3 | 17 hours |
| Week 4 | 19 hours |
| Week 5 | 22 hours |

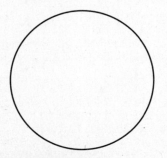

4. Sara bought pencils for $4.00, books for $8.00, and fruit for $4.00. If she had $20.00 at the beginning of the day, how much did she have at the end of the day? Draw a circle graph to show how Sara spent her money. Be sure to give your graph a title. _____

**Graphs: Word Problems**

Math 5, SV 8049-9

**p. 5** 1. 684 2. 37,901 3. 808 4. 60,650 5. $66.66
6. 0.999 7. 14.4 8. 2,166.64 9. 12 10. 5 5/8
11. 1,440,000 12. 68 R 1 13. 5 13/14 14. 4 11/20
15. 5 16. 59.3 17. 4,850 18. 11 1/6 19. 12.08
20. 0.18 21. 187 R 2 22. 132 23. 495 24. 25.68
25. 5,569 26. 0.57

**p. 6** 1. $9.00 2. 68.1 tons 3. 89 students 4. 1,200
breaths 5. 45 mm thick 6. 27 marbles
7. 6,250 cubic feet 8. 2 1/2 yards more

**p. 7** 1. 100,000 + 2,000 + 60; one hundred two thousand,
sixty 2. 200,504,908; two hundred million, five hundred
four thousand, nine hundred eight
3. one hundred million, seventy thousand; 100,000,000 +
70,000 4. 380,962; three hundred eighty thousand, nine
hundred sixty-two 5. 563,400; 500,000 + 60,000 + 3,000
+ 400 6. 70,084,039; 70,000,000 + 80,000 + 4,000 + 30
+ 9 7. 400; 4 hundreds 8. 500,000; 5 hundred thousands
9. 90,000,000; 9 ten millions 10. 900,000,000; 9 hundred
millions 11. $145,987.00; One hundred forty-five
thousand, nine hundred eighty-seven dollars

**p. 8** 1. < 2. > 3. < 4. = 5. < 6. > 7. < 8. = 9. > 10. >
11. 2,345; 2,347; 2,435 12. 743,194; 743,204; 753,194
13. 2,435,657; 2,345,657; 2,345,567 14. 13,467; 13,476;
13,746 15. Oklahoma, Kentucky, Alabama

**p. 9** 1. 30 2. 240 3. 450 4. 6,260 5. 900 6. 1,800
7. 45,800 8. 3,000 9. 24,000 10. 125,000 11. 50,000
12. 120,000 13. 580,000 14. 100,000 15. 1,500,000
16. 2,400,000 17. 57,000,000 18. 156,000,000
19. 2,350; 2,000 20. 125,680; 126,000 21. 1,234,500;
1,234,000 22. no

**p. 10** 1. Students shade 9 columns. 2. Students shade
9 blocks. 3. Students shade 9 blocks. 4. 0.75 5. 4.6
6. 7.12 7. 9.009 8. 300.5 9. 8.472 10. hundredths
11. thousandths 12. tenths 13. thousandths
14. thousandths 15. ones 16. tenths 17. hundredths
18. baseball-0.423; tennis-0.095

**p. 11** 1. > 2. < 3. = 4. = 5. < 6. < 7. 5.12, 5.14, 5.21,
5.41 8. 45.21, 45.32, 46.89, 46.98 9. 0.005, 0.050,
0.505 10. 4.123, 41.23, 41,230 11. 0.95, 0.63, 0.59, 0.58
12. 532.91, 532.90, 432.76, 289.74 13. 4,968, 496.8,
49.68, 4.968 14. 4.536, 4.356, 3.654, 3.456
15. 8.65 16. 2.81 17. oranges

**p. 12** 1. 0.4 2. 0.7 3. 0.24 4. 1 5. 0.4 6. 0.5 7. 12.8
8. 46.4 9. 1,234.7 10. 4,513.8 11. 0.12 12. 0.15
13. 3.55 14. 85.61 15. 175.43 16. 78.47 17. $5.00
18. $15.00 19. $124.00 20. 13 minutes

**p. 13** 1. 0.3 miles 2. $3.40 3. 53.1°F, 59.3°F, 60.4°F,
67.5°F, 68.04°F 4. 93,000,000; 90,000,000 + 3,000,000
5. sixty-eight and four hundredths degrees Fahrenheit

**p. 14** 1. 600 2. 600 3. 6,000 4. 40,000 5. 60,000
6. 2,400 7. 8,000 8. 5,000 9. 22,000 10. 600 11. 800
12. 300 13. 2,000 14. 3,200 15. 3,000 16. 20,000
17. 99,000 18. $26 + $36 + $20 = $82; yes

**p. 15** 1. 60 2. 331 3. 820 4. 163 5. 1,579 6. 2,241
7. 4,332 8. 5,440 9. 30,717 10. 103,012 11. 369,769
12. 727,620 13. 6,057,867 14. 900,073,973
15. 135 + 106 + 116 = 357 feet

**p. 16** 1. 84 2. 257 3. 77 4. 395 5. 382 6. 365
7. 2,778 8. 32,384 9. 21,109 10. 14,436 11. 30,981
12. 5,091 13. 60,650 14. 19,135 15. 228,221

16. 182,752 17. 226,763 18. 736,724,581
19. 88,550 − 87,650 = 900 seats

**p. 17** 1. $14.00 2. 2.00 3. 8.000 4. 424.00 5. 52.000
6. 240.0 7. $67.00 8. 11.00 9. 34.00 10. $1.00
11. 186.00 12. 5,252.0 13. 11.00 14. 316.0 15. 919.00
16. 3.0 17. 19.0 18. $88.00 19. Steve's

**p. 18** 1. 9.9 2. 53.0 3. 36.36 4. 299.59 5. 1.651
6. 4.75 7. 9.64 8. 13.148 9. 35.64 10. 53.29
11. 255.86 12. 352.91 13. 401.742 14. 777.96
15. 100.18 16. 2.70 17. 22.7 18. 37.908
19. $3.75 + $2.75 + $1.35 = $7.85

**p. 19** 1. 2.5 2. 4.3 3. 4.8 4. 10.90 5. 0.64 6. 14.59
7. $64.57 8. 0.033 9. $41.44 10. 0.159 11. 419.76
12. 10.61 13. 3.639 14. 495.3 15. 3.3 16. 5.42
17. 18.599 18. 8.376 19. $30.45 − $17.90 = $12.55

**p. 20** 1. 0.80, 0.8000 2. 1.3, 1.300 3. 3.00, 3.000
4. 6.40, 6.4 5. 1.200 + 4.561 = $n$ 6. 6.45 − 2.00 = $n$
7. 8.70 − 0.02 = $n$ 8. 3.20 + 4.26 = $n$ 9. 25.060 − 9.315
= $n$ 10. 6.546 + 12.800 = $n$ 11. 0.43 + 0.20 = 0.63
12. 0.80 + 0.52 = 1.32 13. 1.42 + 0.50 = 1.92 14. 4.000
+ 23.175 = 27.175 15. 8.10 − 5.73 = 2.37 16. 3.864 −
0.830 = 3.034 17. 86.32 + 72.9 + 54.8 = 214.02 points

**p. 21** 1. 432 2. 0.9 3. 814 4. 56.49 5. 25.68 6. 3,589
7. 28.63 8. 13.65 9. 6,842 10. 10.579 11. 5.631
12. 8.733 13. 374,702 14. 47,439,284 15. 35,136
16. 1.15 17. 223 18. 77.558 19. 28.68 20. 38,844
21. 108.75 − 95.4 = 13.35 pounds

**p. 22** 1. 7,752 miles 2. 73.4 miles 3. 146.445 gallons
of gas 4. A-One Gas; $0.06 per gallon 5. 205,761 miles

**p. 23** 1. 560 2. 3,600 3. 6,000 4. 16,000 5. 540,000
6. 400,000 7. 1,200 8. 40 9. 420 10. 30,000 11. 600
12. 8 13. 60; 600; 6,000 14. 70; 700; 7,000 15. 30; 300;
3,000 16. 500; 5,000; 50,000 17. 900; 9,000; 90,000
18. 500 x 7 = 3,500 pounds

**p. 24** 1. 70 x 2 = 140 2. 40 x 4 = 160 3. 600 x 5 = 3,000
4. 700 x 8 = 5,600 5. 2,000 x 3 = 6,000 6. 500 x 6 =
3,000 7. 6,000 x 7 = 42,000 8. 90 x 40 = 3,600
9. 40 x 20 = 800 10. 70 x 20 = 1,400 11. 700 x 60 =
42,000 12. 400 x 20 = 8,000 13. 600 x 50 = 30,000
14. 246 x 16 = about 4,000 bulbs

**p. 25** 1. 365 2. 174 3. 504 4. 2,718 5. 516 6. 852
7. 16,424 8. 19,536 9. 52,209 10. 28,020 11. 756
12. 45,626 13. 8,460 14. 7,144 15. 329 16. 3,810
17. 11,864 18. 2,142 19. 34,008 20. 5,925
21. 2,200 x 7 = 15,400 miles

**p. 26** 1. 1,464 2. 276 3. 7,544 4. 2,079 5. 3,456
6. 2,790 7. 10,778 8. 12,382 9. 29,376 10. 32,565
11. 32,946 12. 27,636 13. 750,444 14. 119,798
15. 667 16. 17,442 17. 20,370 18. 63,851
19. 40 x 15 = 600 players

**p. 27** 1. 75,582 2. 356,484 3. 379,122 4. 444,906
5. 244,842 6. 216,664 7. 216,192 8. 223,344
9. 375,412 10. 82,622 11. 2,165,187 12. 1,640,688
13. 2,386,752 14. 2,478,132 15. 246 x 365 =
89,790 papers

**p. 28** 1. 1.3 2. 314.0 3. 42.3; 423.0; 4,230.0; 42,300.0
4. 7.81; 78.10; 781.0; 7,810.0 5. 3; 30; 300 6. 62; 620;
6,200 7. 80.4; 804; 8,040 8. 13.1; 131; 1,310 9. 7
10. 40 11. 19.4 12. 6,510 13. 492 14. 8,033
15. 6.7 x 10 = 67 miles

Math 5, SV 8049-9

**p. 29** 1. 76 2. 340 3. 16 4. 112 5. 288 6. 102 7. 195 8. 352 9. 330 10. 249 11. 310 12. 384 13. 144 14. 96 15. 235 16. 18.1 17. R 18. 203.84 19. R 20. R 21. 110.37 22. 52.6 x 6 = about 300 words

**p. 30** 1. 0.21 2. 0.06 For 3.–5., check students' work. 3. 0.21 4. 0.45 5. 0.35 6. 0.06 7. 0.18 8. 0.20 9. 0.72 10. 0.28 11. 0.09 12. 0.4 x 2 = 0.8 inches

**p. 31** 1. 36.4 2. 25.12 3. $79.69 4. 32 5. $49.24 6. 107.75 7. $149.70 8. 26.703 9. $172.41 10. $431.55 11. 62.4 12. 50.4 13. $30.96 14. 9.306 15. 1,300.76 16. 26 x 1.609 = 41.834 kilometers

**p. 32** 1. 0.98 2. 2.88 3. 23.31 4. 29.264 5. 39.644 6. 40.888 7. 131.12 8. 11.4 9. $121.84 10. 1,383.21 11. 0.018 12. 13.455 13. 62.4 14. 60.03 15. 1.28 16. 39.06 17. 0.1 18. 14.595 19. 1,059.48 20. 16.614 21. 13.62 x 5 = 68.1 tons

**p. 33** 1. 516 2. 2,660 3. 7,296 4. 3.5 5. $6.30 6. 1.96 7. 4,260 8. 0.009 9. 48,240 10. 125.764 11. $36.70 12. 2,126,454 13. 1,059.48 14. $56.40 15. 0.015 16. 360,000 17. 33,280 18. $229.95 19. 9 x 0.29 = $2.61

**p. 34** 1. 94,395 people 2. $74.80 3. $0.11; $2.31 4. 320 hours 5. $300

**p. 35** 1. b 2. a 3. a 4. b 5. 8 6. 13 7. 7 8. 6 9. 10 10. 40 11. 16 12. 80 13. 90 14. 110 15. 80 16. 110 17. 7 18. 9 19. 9 20. 22 21. 115 22. 90 23. 90 24. 60 25. 110 26. 63 ÷ 4 = about 16 students

**p. 36** 1. 7 R 2 2. 11 R 1 3. 12 R 2 4. 9 R 6 5. 10 R 1 6. 8 R 3 7. 4 R 4 8. 9 R 4 9. 12 R 2 10. 10 R 3 11. 21 R 3 12. 13 13. 29 R 2 14. 16 R 1 15. 12 16. 23 R 2 17. 5 R 5 18. 8 R 2 19. 10 R 4 20. 9 R 1 21. 10 R 6 22. 5 R 7 23. 1 R 4 24. 12 25. 88 ÷ 22 = 4 tickets

**p. 37** 1. 90 2. 203 3. 100 R 5 4. 77 R 3 5. 79 R 6 6. 153 R 2 7. 124 R 6 8. 156 R 3 9. 483 R 1 10. 4,737 11. 17,551 R 1 12. 22 R 2 13. 23 R 5 14. 107 R 2 15. 84 R 5 16. 591 R 2 17. 7,046 R 5 18. 132 ÷ 4 = 33 people

**p. 38** 1. 2 2. 7 3. 2 4. 30 5. 2 6. 5 7. 100 8. 70 9. 400 10. 2,000 11. 160 ÷ 16 = 10 12. 420 ÷ 60 = 7 13. 250 ÷ 50 = 5 14. 800 ÷ 20 = 40 15. 8,200 ÷ 20 = 400 16. 5,600 ÷ 70 = 80 17. 593 ÷ 64 = about 10 students

**p. 39** For 1.–11. check students' work. 1. 2 2. 1 R 30 3. 5 4. 3 R 3 5. 1 R 19 6. 2 R 32 7. 3 R 5 8. 2 R 13 9. 6 R 9 10. 1 R 29 11. 1 R 16 12. 2 R 29 13. 5 R 1 14. 2 R 8 15. 3 R 2 16. 4 R 12 17. 2 R 9 18. $11 ÷ 3 = 3 R 2; 3 pairs of socks; $2 left

**p. 40** 1. 39 R 16 2. 24 R 12 3. 49 R 16 4. 21 R 3 5. 31 6. 8 R 11 7. 3 R 36 8. 5 9. 14 R 43 10. 91 11. 39 12. 93 13. 1,201 14. 700 R 10 15. 3 cases; 6 more spoons

**p. 41** 1. 61.7 2. 0.036 3. 0.311 4. 0.625 5. 3.7; 0.37; 0.037 6. 21.1; 2.11; 0.211 7. 293.4; 29.34; 2.934 8. 0.39 9. 7.4 10. 2.11 11. 0.217 12. 5.13 13. 0.928 14. 0.64 15. 3.7 16. 1.27 17. 0.816 18. 10.24 19. 0.431 20. 38.9 ÷ 10 = 3.89 yards

**p. 42** 1. 0.7 2. 0.4 3. 0.8 4. 0.03 5. 0.42 6. 3.09 7. 1.05 8. 7.6 9. 1.31 10. 8.03 11. 7.4 12. 7.2 13. 13.2 14. 5.3 15. 0.012 16. 59.3 17. 3.68 18. 2.05 19. 1.32 20. 1.67 21. 0.34 22. 0.57 23. $6.52 ÷ 4 = $1.63

**p. 43** 1. 2 2. 5 3. 8 R 5 4. 3.1 5. 0.4 6. 21 R 3 7. 7.4 8. 2.30 9. 1.75 10. 304 11. 101 12. 721 R 3 13. 20 R 33 14. 104 15. 701 16. 920 17. 5 18. 61 19. 0.098 20. 0.34 21. 12.93 22. 32 23. 36 ÷ 12 = 3 feet

**p. 44** 1. 19 miles 2. Purity 3. 7 cabins 4. no 5. 2 batteries; $0.22

**p. 45** 1. 1/3 2. 1/2 3. 3/4 4. 2/5 5. Check students' drawings. 6. Check students' drawings. 7. 3/12 8. 2/7 9. 2/11

**p. 46** 1. 1/2, 2/4 2. 1/3, 2/6 3. 3/5, 6/10 4. 1/4, 2/8 5. 3 6. 3 7. 10 8. c 9. b 10. a 11. yes; The fraction 1/2 is equivalent to 2/4.

**p. 47** 1. 1, 14, 2, 7 2. 1, 13 3. 1, 36, 2, 18, 3, 12, 4, 9, 6 4. 1, 32, 2, 16, 4, 8 5. 8: 1, 2, 4, 8; 16: 1, 2, 4, 8, 16; common factors: 1, 2, 4, 8 6. 9: 1, 3, 9; 24: 1, 2, 3, 4, 6, 8, 12, 24; common factors: 1, 3 7. 10: 1, 2, 5, 10; 15: 1, 3, 5, 15; common factors: 1, 5 8. 12: 1, 2, 3, 4, 6, 12; 13: 1, 13; common factors: 1 9. 9: 1, 3, 9; 27: 1, 3, 9, 27; greatest common factor: 9 10. 12: 1, 2, 3, 4, 6, 12; 18: 1, 2, 3, 6, 9, 18; greatest common factor: 6 11. 13: 1, 13; 39: 1, 3, 13, 39; greatest common factor: 13 12. 14: 1, 2, 7, 14; 21: 1, 3, 7, 21; greatest common factor: 7 13. no

**p. 48** 1. yes 2. no 3. yes 4. yes 5. no 6. no 7. 1/5 8. 1/5 9. 3/5 10. 1/3 11. 1/3 12. 1/2 13. 1/6 14. 2/3 15. 7/8 16. 1/3 17. 2/7

**p. 49** 1. Possible answer: 4, 8, 12 2. Possible answer: 5, 10, 15 3. Possible answer: 12, 24 4. Possible answer: 18, 36 5. 16 6. 10 7. 15 8. 12 9. 15 10. 6 11. 45 12. 20 13. 12 14. 90 15. 15 16. 20 17. 18 18. 30 19. 40 20. 18 21. 35 22. 8 23. 18 beads

**p. 50** For 1.–3. check students' answers. 4. = 5. < 6. < 7. > 8. < 9. = 10. > 11. = 12. > 13. = 14. > 15. > 16. < 17. = 18. 1/3, 3/6, 2/3 19. 1/8, 2/4, 6/8 20. 1/4, 1/2, 7/12 21. 2/5, 1/3, 4/15 22. 3/8, 5/16, 1/4 23. 9/10, 4/5, 1/2 24. blueberries

**p. 51** 1. 1 2. 1 1/2 3. 1 2/3 4. 2 3/8 5. 1 1/4 6. 1 4/5 7. 1 4/6 or 1 2/3 8. 3 9. 35/8 10. 7/2 11. 7/3 12. 39/4 13. 3 1/4, 3 1/3, 3 7/8 14. 2 1/9, 2 3/5, 4 1/9 15. Students draw 4 whole sandwiches cut in halves and 1/2 of another sandwich.

**p. 52** 1. 1 – 3/4 = 1/4 2. 4/8 + 2/8 = 6/8 or 3/4 3. 7/8 4. 2/3 5. 7/8 6. 1/2 7. 3/4 8. 1/2 9. 2/5 10. 4/5 11. 5/6 12. 1/2 13. 1 14. 1/3 15. 3/7 16. 1/3 17. 1 hour

**p. 53** 1. yes 2. yes 3. no 4. no 5. yes 6. no 7. yes 8. yes 9. no 10. no 11. yes 12. yes 13. no 14. no 15. 2/6, 1/6 16. 5/6, 2/6 17. 7/8, 6/8 18. 9/10, 2/10 19. 2/9, 3/9 20. 3/6, 2/6 21. 7/28, 8/28 22. 15/30, 6/30 23. 2/6, 2/6 24. 15/60 or 1/4 hour

**p. 54** 1. 8/15 2. 7/10 3. 11/20 4. 5/6 5. 3/8 6. 1/4 7. 3/10 8. 9/20 9. 2/3 10. 1/20 11. 13/15 12. 5/8 13. 13/14 14. 3/8 15. 2/3 16. 1/2 17. 1/10 18. 1 1/6 19. 1/4 20. 3/4 – 3/8 = 3/8 yard

**p. 55** 1. 6 7/8 2. 2/3 3. 7 5/8 4. 1 1/2 5. 1 5/9 6. 5 7. 2 4/5 8. 8 3/8 9. 6 1/2 10. 4 7/8 11. 4 7/8 12. 2 8/11 13. 6 1/2 14. 6 15. 3 2/5 16. 4 2/3 17. 2 3/4 + 2 1/4 = 5 bags

**p. 56** 1. 1/2 2. 12 1/10 3. 15 2/9 4. 1 8/9 5. 16 3/20 6. 2 1/3 7. 12 1/6 8. 5/8 9. 5 13/14 10. 9 1/2 11. 1 11/12 12. 8 1/12 13. 8 1/8 14. 4 4/9 15. 11 5/6 16. 3 5/8 17. 10 18. 1 1/4 19. 16 5/16 20. 3 3/8 21. 15 5/6 – 11 2/3 = 4 1/6 feet

**p. 57** 1. 1/2 x 4 = 2 2. 2/3 x 6 = 4 3. 1/4 x 12 = 3 4. 1/3 x 9 = 3 5. 5 6. 8 7. 9 8. 9 9. 4 10. 2 1/3 11. 1 3/5 12. 7 13. 6 1/4 14. 4 15. 4 4/5 16. 2 1/4 17. 500 x 2/5 = 200 boxes

Math 5, SV 8049-9

**p. 58** 1. 5/8 x 2/3 = 5/12  2. 1/10 x 5/6 = 5/60 or 1/12  3. 3/8  4. 2/27  5. 2/25  6. 1/10  7. 1/34  8. 1/12  9. 1/27  10. 9/100  11. 5/36  12. 4/27  13. 3/16  14. 1/7  15. 4/15  16. 3/14  17. 5/16  18. 3/4 x 2/3 = 6/12 or 1/2 yard

**p. 59** 1. 8/3 x 3 2/3 = 9 7/9  2. 3/4 x 2 2/3 = 2  3. 8/9  4. 1 11/16  5. 1 1/16  6. 2 5/8  7. 1  8. 15/16  9. 3/5  10. 1 11/21  11. 11/14  12. 6 1/4 x 2/5 = 2 1/2 dozen

**p. 60** 1. 5 fives  2. 3 fours  3. 4 threes  4. 8/10 ÷ 4/10 = 2  5. 12/3 ÷ 2/3 = 6  6. 6/8 ÷ 2/8 = 3  7. 2  8. 2  9. 3  10. 2  11. 3  12. 1  13. 3  14. 1  15. 3  16. 4  17. 3  18. 5  19. 4 valentines

**p. 61** 1. 5/6  2. 3/5  3. 1/2  4. 1  5. 4 8/9  6. 4 5/8  7. 1 4/15  8. 8  9. 9 1/4  10. 7 1/2  11. 4 11/20  12. 7  13. 1/4  14. 15/16  15. 2  16. 8 1/12  17. 1 1/2  18. 3/8  19. 5 13/14  20. 10 1/4  21. 1 3/4  22. 6  23. 2 3/4 + 1 2/3 = 4 5/12 inches

**p. 62** 1. 5 hours  2. 10 1/4 hours  3. 6 students  4. 15/60 or 1/4 hour  5. 3 1/6 pages

**p. 63** 1. b  2. c  3. a  4. 8 cm, 84 mm  5. 11 cm, 111 mm  6. 10 cm, 102 mm  7. 23.2 cm

**p. 64** 1. a  2. b  3. a  4. b  5. L  6. mL  7. L  8. L  9. mL  10. L  11. mL  12. L  13. 0.0505  14. 406,200  15. 4 scoops

**p. 65** 1. kilograms  2. grams  3. grams  4. kilograms  5. a  6. b  7. 17 portions  8. 8 portions  9. 24 portions  10. 20 portions  11. 65 x 12 = 780 grams

**p. 66** 1. 2 3/8 in.  2. 1 3/4 in.  3. 4 1/2 in.  4. 2 1/16 in. For 5.–8. check students' drawings.  9. 24  10. 2,640  11. 150  12. 2  13. 880  14. 4  15. 3  16. 3  17. 3  18. Bayard is taller. 5 3/4 − 5 9/16 = 3/16 inch

**p. 67** 1. multiply  2. divide  3. multiply  4. divide  5. divide  6. multiply  7. 6  8. 48  9. 14  10. 32  11. 12  12. 11  13. 16  14. 24  15. 16  16. 32  17. 8  18. 3  19. 68  20. 2 1/2  21. 13,000  22. 16 x 2.5 = 40 glasses

**p. 68** 1. 48  2. 168  3. 9  4. 600  5. 21  6. 730  7. 3  8. 360  9. 13  10. 8, 18  11. 202  12. 7, 47  13. 1, 146  14. 5, 2  15. 17, 4  16. 17,520  17. 1, 48  18. 4  19. 604,800  20. 180 x 3 = 540 hours

**p. 69** 1. 6:40 A.M.  2. 11:38 A.M.  3. 6:17 P.M.  4. Friday, 3:41 A.M.  5. 2 hr 28 min  6. 10 min 16 sec  7. 3 min 33 sec  8. 9 hr 3 min  9. 44 sec  10. 3 hr 26 min  11. 1 hr 55 min

**p. 70** 1. 2 pounds 13 ounces  2. 6:35  3. 124 grams  4. 8 pints for $2.00  5. 25.7 kilometers

**p. 71** 1. b  2. a  3. b  4. a  5. Main Street

**p. 72** 1. acute  2. right  3. obtuse  4. 50°  5. 110°  6. 90°  7. 70° For 8.–13. check students' drawings.  14. acute

**p. 73** 1. quadrilateral  2. quadrilateral  3. octagon  4. triangle  5. Students circle the triangle, hexagon, square, and octagon. For 6.–9. check students' drawings.  6. parallelogram  7. square  8. rhombus  9. trapezoid  10. Yes; A square is a special rectangle with sides that are all the same length.

**p. 74** 1. scalene  2. isosceles  3. equilateral  4. isosceles  5. right  6. acute  7. right  8. obtuse  9. Yes; An equilateral triangle has three acute angles.

**p. 75** 1. never  2. always  3. always  4. sometimes  5. point *m*  6. Possible answers include radii *MA, MT, MH*  7. *AH*  8. diameter  9. point *S*  10. radius  11. diameter  12. 16 feet

**p. 76** 1. yes  2. no  3. no  4. yes For 5.–10. check students' drawings.  11. F, G, J, K, L  12. A, B, C, D, E, M

**p. 77** 1. Check students' drawing.  2. Check students' drawing.  3. slide  4. turn  5. flip  6. yes  7. no  8. yes  9. Check students' drawing.  10. slide

**p. 78** 1. hexagonal prism V-12, E-18, F-8  2. triangular pyramid V-4, E-6, F-4  3. cube V-8, E-12, F-6  4. triangular prism V-6, E-9, F-5  5. rectangular prism V-8, E-12, F-6  6. 2 circles, 1 rectangle  7. 1 square, 4 triangles  8. 6 rectangles  9. square pyramid

**p. 79** 1. 24 m  2. 24 mm  3. 28 m  4. 57 ft  5. 40 cm  6. 28 ft  7. 50 m  8. 36 ft  9. 7 in.  10. 30 yd  11. 7 ft  12. 60 in.

**p. 80** 1. 70.0 mm  2. 48.7 mm  3. 56.2 mm  4. 89.5 mm  5. 26.9 cm  6. 8.2 cm  7. 60.4 cm  8. 42.7 cm  9. 75.0 cm  10. 23 ft 3 1/2 in x 3.14 = 878 in.

**p. 81** 1. 108 cm$^2$  2. 176 cm$^2$  3. 36 in.$^2$  4. 51 m$^2$  5. 78 in$^2$  6. 750 mm$^2$  7. 900 mm$^2$  8. 110 mm$^2$  9. 25 x 35 = 875 ft$^2$

**p. 82** 1. 6 cm$^2$  2. 8 cm$^2$  3. 8 mi$^2$  4. 18 m$^2$  5. 4 cm$^2$  6. 63.0 in.$^2$  7. 48 m$^2$  8. 85 ft$^2$  9. 14 ft$^2$  10. 21 ft$^2$  11. 36 in.$^2$  12. (120 x 48) ÷ 2 = 2,880 m$^2$

**p. 83** 1. 112 yd$^2$  2. 252 cm$^2$  3. 80 m$^2$  4. 160 ft$^2$  5. 28 mm$^2$  6. 18 mm$^2$  7. Joy, 100 ft$^2$ bigger

**p. 84** 1. 18 cubes  2. 27 cubes  3. 14 cubes  4. 24 cubes  5. 18 cubes  6. 12 cubes  7. 14 cubes  8. 4  9. 3, 5, 6  10. 64 cubes, yes

**p. 85** 1. 63 cm$^3$  2. 72 cm$^3$  3. 40 cm$^3$  4. 72 cm$^3$  5. 60 cm$^3$  6. 64 cm$^3$  7. 15,000 ft$^3$  8. 882 in.$^3$  9. 280 in.$^3$  10. 1,000 ft$^3$  11. 12,500 yd$^3$  12. 5 x 4 x 2 x 4 = 160 dm$^3$

**p. 86** 1. 40 ft  2. 94.2 in.  3. 2,400 in.$^3$  4. about 23 cm$^2$  5. triangular pyramid

**p. 87** 1. data, predict  2. survey  3. random  4. Possible answer: The random group would better predict choices, since it is more likely to represent adults whose interests are varied.  5. Answers will vary. Check students' work.

**p. 88** 1. Ben and Anil  2. Crissy  3. 85 votes  4. 135 votes  5. 12 1/2 symbols

**p. 89** 1. Each vertical line represents 20 more trucks.  2. January  3. 50 trucks  4. April  5. Answers will vary. Check students' work.

**p. 90** 1. noon  2. 10 A.M. and 11 A.M.  3. about 9°F  4. between 7 A.M. and 8 A.M. or between 8 A.M. and 9 A.M.  5. Check students' work.

**p. 91** 1. After-School Activities of 40 Students  2. The graph is labeled with 3 activities and the number of students participating.  3. Half as many students prefer television viewing as sports.  4. Check students' work. The graph should be divided into thirds.  5. Check students' work. The graph should show 2/3 with 18 bulbs blooming and 1/3 with 9 bulbs not blooming.

**p. 92** 1. (3, 4)  2. (6, 1)  3. (4, 3)  4. (3, 5)  5. Art  6. Claire  7. Ellen  8. Denny  9. rectangle, Check students' work.  10. Check students' work.

**p. 93** 1. 76 people  2. Check students' work.  3. 32 hours  4. Check students' work. The circle graph should show: Pencils, 1/5, $4.00; Books, 2/5, $8.00; Fruit, 1/5, $4.00; Money Left, 1/5, $4.00

Math 5, SV 8049-9